WITHDRAWN

ECONOMICS AND ECONOMIC SYSTEMS

ECONOMICS
TAKING THE MYSTERY OUT OF MONEY

ECONOMICS AND ECONOMIC SYSTEMS

EDITED BY BRIAN DUIGNAN,
SENIOR EDITOR, RELIGION AND PHILOSOPHY

Britannica
Educational Publishing

IN ASSOCIATION WITH

ROSEN
EDUCATIONAL SERVICES

Published in 2013 by Britannica Educational Publishing
(a trademark of Encyclopædia Britannica, Inc.)
in association with Rosen Educational Services, LLC
29 East 21st Street, New York, NY 10010.

First Edition

Britannica Educational Publishing
J.E. Luebering: Senior Manager
Marilyn L. Barton: Senior Coordinator, Production Control
Steven Bosco: Director, Editorial Technologies
Lisa S. Braucher: Senior Producer and Data Editor
Yvette Charboneau: Senior Copy Editor
Kathy Nakamura: Manager, Media Acquisition
Brian Duignan, Senior Editor, Religion and Philosophy

Rosen Educational Services
Nicholas Croce: Editor
Nelson Sá: Art Director
Cindy Reiman: Photography Manager
Marty Levick: Photo Researcher
Brian Garvey: Designer, Cover Design
Introduction by John Strazzabosco

Library of Congress Cataloging-in-Publication Data

Economics and economic systems/edited by Brian Duignan.—1st ed.
    p. cm.—(Economics: taking the mystery out of money)
"In association with Britannica Educational Publishing, Rosen Educational Services."
Includes bibliographical references and index.
ISBN 978-1-61530-892-7 (library binding)
1. Economics. I. Duignan, Brian.
HB171.E2486 2013
330—dc23
                                                                    2012022528

Manufactured in the United States of America

On the cover: A stock chart. © *iStockphoto.com/Danil Melekhin*

Cover (background), pp. i, iii, 1, 6, 24, 41, 64, 78, 93, 103, 114 zphoto/Shutterstock.com

CONTENTS

ix

10

42

46

79

83

97

107

INTRODUCTION

People have tried to define "economics" for centuries, but it's proven to be an elusive concept. Despite the difficulty in defining it, experts have long agreed that economics deals with certain basic premises. Economics is the social science concerned primarily with the study and explanation of the production, distribution, and consumption of goods and services.

Economics as we know it has its roots in the eighteenth century. In 1776, Scottish philosopher Adam Smith published *An Inquiry into the Nature and Causes of the Wealth of Nations*. Smith's book is about economic growth and the policies that can encourage or deter it. Smith recommended economic policies that would promote competition among private businesses. His ideas formed the foundation of classical political economy.

Englishman David Ricardo published *Principles of Political Economy and Taxation* in 1817, in which he introduced the concept of the economic model. Ricardo's theories centred on the idea that economic growth will eventually be obstructed by the rising cost of cultivating food on limited land.

German philosopher Karl Marx is often considered the last of the classical economists. Marxian economics posits that value and profits are a result of human labour alone. This idea was often used to criticize the class divisions that arise from capitalism.

In the late 1800s, economists from Austria, England, and France initiated a revolution in economic thinking. These economists became known as marginalists. This name comes from their marginal utility theory of value, which attempted to explain prices on the basis of the behaviour of consumers in choosing among increments of goods and services.

Modern economics continued to evolve during the 20th century. One of the greatest contributions came from

Statue of Adam Smith, Edinburgh, Scotland. Jason Friend/Radius Images/Getty Images

English economist John Maynard Keynes. Today Keynes is considered one of the founders of macroeconomics, the branch of economics that is concerned with national or regional economies as a whole.

Economists often distinguish between "positive" economics and "normative" economics. The former strives to describe and explain the facts of an economy without making value judgments. The latter, on the other hand, expresses judgments about the desirability of different economic policies.

Economic theories begin as theoretical models, which are simplified descriptions of patterns of real-world economic activity. By manipulating a model, economists can make predictions and compare their findings to the real world. Their predictions, however, are at best probable or likely and never certain. It's difficult to test economic theories. The theories can never be proven to be true, but they can be proven false by new data. Economists can predict the effects of specific changes in the economy. However, they're better at forecasting the direction of events, rather than the size of the outcome.

There are two main branches of economic theory. As previously stated, macroeconomics is the study of national economies as a whole. Microeconomics addresses the economy as if it were made up of businesses and households only. The aim of microeconomics is to say something meaningful about the forces that influence supply and demand.

There are numerous fields within contemporary economics. Money has been one of the main fields in economics for hundreds of years. In the 19th century, the quantity theory of money grew in importance. This theory states that inflation or deflation can be controlled by changing the quantity of money in circulation. Keynes challenged this traditional theory in the 1930s, arguing that changes in government budgetary and tax policies are more effective. Since then, Keynesian economics and the quantity theory of money have each experienced revivals.

Development economics is recognized as one of the three main subfields of economics, along with microeconomics and macroeconomics. This field seeks to explain changes in economic systems over time. Researchers in the highly technical field of economic growth create economic modelsto study the processes through which a nation's wealth increases.

International economics seeks to understand the flow of goods and services between nations. It also deals with the effects of changes to the exchange rate of a currency. The field of labour economics is concerned with the labour force as an element in the process of production. Other fields include public finance, industrial organization, agriculture, law and economics, information economics, and financial economics.

It might seem like numerous economic systems must exist given the many cultures that have existed throughout history, one might think that numerous economic systems must exist now. In fact, however, there are only three types of economic system: those based on the principle of tradition, those organized according to command, and market economies. Each form focuses on the economic problem of production and distribution.

Primitive economies developed around the principle of tradition. This type of system still exists today in some cultures, such as the Bedouin peoples of the Middle Eastern deserts. Characteristics of a traditional economy may include hunting and gathering, migration due to climate, and slash-and-burn agriculture.

As societies grew stronger, the command system rose to prominence. Command systems in ancient societies—such as those that developed in Egypt, China, India, and the Americas—were characterized by the ability of centralized authority to take large numbers of people away from traditional systems and use the labour force to do work for a small number of elite leaders. This type of system led to numerous technological advances, such as the construction of the pyramids in Egypt. In time, command became the main organizing principle for socialistic economies.

In both traditional and command systems, economic activities are tied directly to the activities that define the cultures in which they function. Unlike traditional economic systems, however, command economies are capable of creating enormous surpluses.

The market system differs from the previous two. It's based on the concept of supply and demand and is designed to encourage individuals to improve their material and financial standing through economic practices.

Marketplaces have existed for thousands of years, but market economies did not come into existence until the 17th and 18th centuries. The rise of market systems can be understood by following the development of capitalism. The earliest form of capitalism was mercantilism.

European nations began striving to strengthen state power at the expense of rival nations. Precious metals, for example, were often obtained through trade with foreign nations. Mercantilist practices included setting up ports and colonies in foreign lands and forbidding colonies from trading with foreign nations. These early practices foreshadowed the rise of modern capitalistic policies.

Traders complained that governments had created monopolies that guaranteed exclusive trading rights to a small number of companies. They wanted an economic system in which the production and distribution of goods and services were accomplished through market forces and in which levels of wages were also determined by supply and demand, not by the ruling elite. In *Wealth of Nations*, Adam Smith argued that the government's role should be limited to national defense, protecting citizens from each other, and the creation and maintenance of public institutions, such as education, that cannot be adequately provided by private businesses. Under Smith's market system, citizens would have the freedom to help shape the processes of production and distribution.

As the Industrial Revolution gained momentum, commercial capitalism proved to be a transitional phase in the development of industrial capitalism. The mechanization and industrialization of productive processes greatly changed the economic system while changing social institutions at the same time. Technological advances in agriculture, iron manufacture, and machine-tool design, among many other areas, began to transform capitalism in the late 18th century.

Soon, the factory became the focus of economic production. Workforces increased greatly. Thanks to modern inventions such as the steam engine, companies that once employed 10 workers quickly expanded to include hundreds and even thousands of employees.

This rise of industrial capitalism created a gulf between the owners and managers of industrial enterprises and the men, women, and children who worked for them. Working conditions were often poor and dangerous. Many workers toiled long hours for little pay. Additionally, the increase of factories changed the physical landscape. Urban squalor, overcrowding, and smog-producing smokestacks became commonplace, resulting in much criticism aimed at capitalism and the business elite.

Economic instability plagued capitalistic nations in the late 1800s and early 1900s. Many smaller companies merged to form cartels and trusts in an attempt to limit economic problems. These efforts did little to halt speculative panics. Depressions became a recurring problem for many nations. The Great Depression of the 1930s affected all capitalist nations. Many explanations of these difficulties have been proposed, including the intrinsic instability of capitalist economies and the failure of government policy.

In the early 20th century industrial capitalism was transformed into state capitalism, characterized by an enlargement in size and functions of the public realm. The rise of industrial trusts led to legislation called antitrust laws to halt monopolistic practices. Amid the Great Depression, new laws were enacted to provide old-age pensions, relief for the poor, and unemployment benefits. These are practices, intended to guarantee the public well-being, that Adam Smith failed to predict.

Economists believe that capitalism will continue to change to meet new developments in society. For example, economic barriers caused by global distances are rapidly becoming inconsequential in light of modern technology. A problematic result of modern technology is the displacement of manufacturing jobs in Europe and North America to regions of Asia, Africa, and South America.

Although capitalism is known to encourage economic growth, there are several notable criticisms of this economic system. As previously mentioned, capitalism has historically proven to be inherently unstable. Another common criticism of capitalism is that it creates great inequalities of wealth between different classes of society.

Modern equivalents of command economic systems spread across the globe in the 1900s, and some still exist today. Generally, these systems are grouped under the term "socialism," which describes an economy controlled by the public or the state in order, ideally, to best serve the entire population.

In the early 1900s, Vladimir Ilich Lenin—founder of the Communist Party of the Soviet Union (CPSU)—proposed a socialist economy that would rely on central collection points from which goods could be delivered to citizens based on their needs. After the Russian Revolution of 1917, Lenin realized that his plan could not be easily implemented. As a result, he partially reinstated capitalism.

After Lenin's death, Joseph Stalin rose to power in the Soviet Union and abandoned the previous leader's capitalistic policies. Under his policy of collectivism, prosperous peasants were forced to give up their farms and join collective farms. Collectivism would dominate the Russian economy for the next 50 years.

Despite rapid technological advancements, the communist economy eventually failed. In the 1980s, Russian president Mikhail Gorbachev began a reorganization of the Russian economy. The new system greatly reduced the role of central planning and encouraged the development of small private enterprises. In 1991 the CPSU disintegrated and the Soviet Union was dissolved. Many of the former Soviet republics turned to capitalism as a means of improving their economies.

Nature and Scope of Economics

Economics is the social science that seeks to analyze and describe the production, distribution, and consumption of wealth. In the 19th century economics was the hobby of gentlemen of leisure and the vocation of a few academics; economists wrote about economic policy but were rarely consulted by legislators before decisions were made. Today there is hardly a government, international agency, or large commercial bank that does not have its own staff of economists. Many

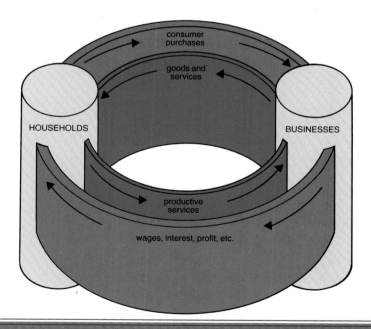

Diagram illustrating the flow of money, goods, and services in a modern industrial economy. Encyclopædia Britannica, Inc.

of the world's economists devote their time to teaching economics in colleges and universities around the world, but most work in various research or advisory capacities, either for themselves (in economics consulting firms), in industry, or in government. Still others are employed in accounting, commerce, marketing, and business administration; although they are trained as economists, their occupational expertise falls within other fields. Indeed, this can be considered "the age of economists," and the demand for their services seems insatiable.

No one has ever succeeded in neatly defining the scope of economics. Many have agreed with Alfred Marshall, a leading 19th-century English economist, that economics is "a study of mankind in the ordinary business of life; it examines that part of individual and social action which is most closely connected with the attainment, and with the use of the material requisites of wellbeing"—ignoring the fact that sociologists, psychologists, and anthropologists frequently study exactly the same phenomena. In the 20th century, the English economist Lionel Robbins defined economics as "the science which studies human behaviour as a relationship between (given) ends and scarce means which have alternative uses." In other words, Robbins said that economics is the science of economizing. While his definition captures one of the striking characteristics of the economist's way of thinking, it is at once too wide (because it would include in economics the game of chess) and too narrow (because it would exclude the study of the national income or the price level). Perhaps the only foolproof definition is that attributed to Canadian-born economist Jacob Viner: economics is what economists do.

Difficult as it may be to define economics, it is not difficult to indicate the sorts of questions that concern economists. Among other things, they seek to analyze the forces determining prices—not only the prices of goods and services but the prices of the resources used to produce them. This involves the discovery of two key elements: what governs the way in which human labour, machines, and land are combined in production and how buyers and sellers are brought together in a functioning market. Because prices of the various things must be interrelated, economists therefore ask how such a "price system" or "market mechanism" hangs together and what conditions are necessary for its survival.

These questions are representative of microeconomics, the part of economics that deals with the behaviour of individual entities such as consumers, business firms, traders, and farmers. The other major

Farming is one part of the economy that falls under the area of microeconomics. iStockphoto/Thinkstock

branch of economics is macroeconomics, which focuses attention on aggregates such as the level of income in the whole economy, the volume of total employment, the flow of total investment, and so forth. Here economists are concerned with the forces determining the income of a country or the level of total investment, and they seek to learn why full employment is so rarely attained and what public policies might help a country achieve higher employment or greater price stability.

But these examples still do not exhaust the range of problems that economists consider. There is also the important field of development economics, which examines the attitudes and institutions supporting the process of economic development in poor countries as well as those capable of self-sustained economic growth (for example, development economics was at the heart of the Marshall Plan, the program of U.S. economic aid to the countries of western Europe in 1948–51). In this field the economist is concerned with the extent to which the factors affecting economic development can be manipulated by public policy.

Cutting across these major divisions in economics are the specialized fields of public finance, money and banking, international trade, labour economics, agricultural economics, industrial organization, and others. Economists are frequently consulted to assess the effects of governmental measures such as taxation, minimum-wage laws, rent controls, tariffs, changes in interest rates, changes in government budgets, and so on.

MARKET

A market is a means by which buyers and sellers are brought into contact with each other and goods and services are exchanged. The term originally referred to a place where products were bought and sold; today a market is any arena, however abstract or far-reaching, in which buyers and sellers make transactions. The commodity exchanges in London and New York, for example, are international markets in which dealers communicate by telephone and computer links as well as through direct contact. Markets trade not only in tangible commodities such as grain and livestock but also in financial instruments such as securities and currencies.

Classical economists developed the theory of perfect competition, in which they imagined free markets as places where large numbers of buyers and sellers communicated easily with each other and traded in commodities that were readily transferable; prices in such markets were determined only by supply and demand. Since the 1930s, economists have focused more often on the theory of imperfect competition, in which supply and demand are not the only factors that influence the operations of the market. In imperfect competition the number of sellers or buyers is limited, rival products are differentiated (by design, quality, brand name, etc.), and various obstacles hinder new producers' entry into the market.

HISTORY OF ECONOMICS

The effective birth of economics as a separate discipline may be traced to the year 1776, when the Scottish philosopher Adam Smith published *An Inquiry into the Nature and Causes of the Wealth of Nations*. There was, of course, economics before Smith: the Greeks made significant contributions, as did the medieval Scholastics, and from the 15th to the 18th century an enormous amount of pamphlet literature discussed and developed the implications of economic nationalism (a body of thought now known as mercantilism). It was Smith, however, who wrote the first full-scale treatise on economics and, by his magisterial influence, founded what later generations were to call the "English school of classical political economy," known today as classical economics.

THE UNINTENDED EFFECTS OF MARKETS

The Wealth of Nations, as its title suggests, is essentially a book about economic development and the policies that can either promote or hinder it. In its practical aspects the book is an attack on the protectionist doctrines of the mercantilists and a brief for the merits of free trade. But in the course of attacking "false doctrines of political economy," Smith essentially analyzed the workings of the private enterprise system as a governor of human activity. He observed that in a "commercial society" each individual is driven by self-interest and can exert only a negligible influence on prices. That is, each person takes prices as they come and is free only to vary the quantities bought and sold at the given prices. The sum of all individuals' separate actions, however, is what ultimately determines prices. The "invisible hand" of competition, Smith implied, assures a social result that is independent of individual intentions and thus creates the possibility of an objective science of economic behaviour. Smith believed that he had found, in competitive markets, an instrument capable of converting "private vices" (such as selfishness) into "public virtues" (such as maximum production). But this is true only if the competitive system is embedded in an appropriate legal and institutional framework—an insight that Smith developed at length but that was largely overlooked by later generations. Even so, this is not the only value of the *Wealth of Nations*, and within Smith's discussion of how nations became rich can be found a simple theory of value, a crude theory of distribution, and primitive theories of international trade and of money. Their imperfections notwithstanding, these theories became the building blocks of classical and modern economics. In fact, the book's prolific nature strengthened its impact because so much was left for Smith's followers to clarify.

CONSTRUCTION OF A SYSTEM

One generation after the publication of Smith's tome, David Ricardo wrote *Principles of Political Economy and*

Taxation (1817). This book acted, in one sense, as a critical commentary on the *Wealth of Nations*. Yet in another sense, Ricardo's work gave an entirely new twist to the developing science of political economy. Ricardo invented the concept of the economic model—a tightly knit logical apparatus consisting of a few strategic variables—that was capable of yielding, after some manipulation and the addition of a few empirically observable extras, results of enormous practical import. At the heart of the Ricardian system is the notion that economic growth must sooner or later be arrested because of the rising cost of cultivating food on a limited land area. An essential ingredient of this argument is the Malthusian principle—enunciated in Thomas Malthus's *Essay on Population* (1798): according to Malthus, as the labour force increases, extra food to feed the extra mouths can be produced only by extending cultivation to less fertile soil or by applying capital and labour to land already under cultivation—with dwindling results because of the so-called law of diminishing returns. Although wages are held down, profits do not rise proportionately, because tenant farmers outbid each other for superior land. As land prices were increasing, Malthus concluded, the chief beneficiaries of economic progress were the landowners.

Since the root of the problem, according to Ricardo, was the declining yield (i.e., bushels of wheat) per unit of land, one obvious solution was to import cheap wheat from other countries. Eager to show that Britain would benefit from specializing in manufactured goods and exporting them in return for food, Ricardo hit upon the "law of comparative costs" as proof of his model of free trade. He assumed that within a given country labour and capital are free to move in search of the highest returns but that between countries they are not. Ricardo showed that the benefits of international trade are determined by a comparison of costs within each country rather than by a comparison of costs between countries. International trade will profit a country that specializes in the production of the goods it can produce relatively more efficiently (the same country would import everything else). For example, India might be able to produce everything more efficiently than England, but India might profit most by concentrating its resources on textiles, in which its efficiency is relatively greater than in other areas of Indian production, and by importing British capital goods. The beauty of the argument is that if all countries take full advantage of this territorial division of labour, total world output is certain to be physically larger than it will be if some or all countries try to become self-sufficient. Ricardo's law, known as the doctrine of comparative advantage, became the fountainhead of 19th-century free trade doctrine.

The influence of Ricardo's treatise was felt almost as soon as it was published, and for over half a century the Ricardian system dominated economic thinking in Britain. In 1848 John Stuart Mill's restatement of Ricardo's thought in his *Principles of Political Economy* brought it new authority for another generation. After 1870, however, most economists slowly turned away from Ricardo's concerns and began to reexamine the foundations of the theory of value—that is, to explain why goods exchange at the prices that they do. As a result, many of the late 19th-century economists devoted their efforts to the problem of how resources are allocated under conditions of perfect competition.

MARXISM

Before proceeding, it is important to discuss the last of the classical economists, Karl Marx. The first volume of his work *Das Kapital* appeared in 1867; after his

Karl Marx. Henry Guttmann/Hulton Archive/Getty Images

death the second and third volumes were published in 1885 and 1894, respectively. If Marx may be called "the last of the classical economists," it is because to a large extent he founded his economics not in the real world but on the teachings of Smith and Ricardo. They had espoused a "labour theory of value," which holds that products exchange roughly in proportion to the labour costs incurred in producing them. Marx worked out all the logical implications of this theory and added to it "the theory of surplus value," which rests on the axiom that human labour alone creates all value and hence constitutes the sole source of profits.

To say that one is a Marxian economist is, in effect, to share the value judgment that it is socially undesirable for some people in the community to derive their income merely from the ownership of property. Since few professional economists in the 19th century accepted this ethical postulate and most were indeed inclined to find some social justification for the existence of private property and the income derived from it, Marxian economics failed to win resounding acceptance among professional economists. The Marxian approach, moreover, culminated in three generalizations about capitalism: the tendency of the rate of profit to fall, the growing impoverishment of the working class, and the increasing severity of business cycles, with the first being the linchpin of all the others.

However, Marx's exposition of the "law of the declining rate of profit" is invalid—both practically and logically (even avid Marxists admit its logical flaws)—and with it all of Marx's other predictions collapse. In addition, Marxian economics had little to say on the practical problems that are the bread and butter of economists in any society, such as the effect of taxes on specific commodities or that of a rise in the rate of interest on the level of total investment. Although Marx's ideas launched social change around the world, the fact remains that Marx had relatively little effect on the development of economics as a social science.

THE MARGINALISTS

The next major development in economic theory, the marginal revolution, stemmed essentially from the work of three individuals: the English logician and economist Stanley Jevons, the Austrian economist Carl Menger, and the French-born economist Léon Walras. Their contribution to economic theory was the replacement of the labour theory of value with the "marginal utility theory of value." The marginalists based their explanation of prices on the behaviour of consumers in choosing among increments of goods and services; that is, they examined the benefit (utility) that a consumer derives from buying an additional unit of something (a commodity or service) that he already possesses in some quantity. The idea of emphasizing the "marginal" (or last) unit proved in the long run to be more significant than the concept of utility alone, because utility measures only the amount of satisfaction derived from a particular economic activity, such as consumption. Indeed, it was the consistent application of marginalism that marked the true dividing line between classical theory and modern economics. The classical economists identified the major economic problem as predicting the effects of changes in the quantity of capital and labour on the rate of growth of national output. The marginal approach, however, focused on the conditions under which these factors tend to be allocated with optimal results among competing uses—optimal in the sense of maximizing consumers' satisfaction.

Through the last three decades of the 19th century, economists of the Austrian, English, and French schools formulated their own interpretations of the marginal revolution. The Austrian school dwelt on the importance of utility as the determinant of value and dismissed classical economics as completely outmoded. The Austrian economist Eugen von Böhm-Bawerk applied the new ideas to the determination of the rate of interest, an important development in capital theory.

The English school, led by Alfred Marshall, sought to reconcile their work with the doctrines of the classical writers. Marshall based his argument on the observation that the classical economists concentrated their efforts on the supply side in the market while the marginal utility theorists were concerned with the demand side. In suggesting that prices are determined by both supply and demand, Marshall famously used the paradigm of a pair of scissors, which cuts with both blades. Seeking to be practical, he applied his "partial equilibrium analysis" to particular markets and industries.

It was Léon Walras, though, living in the French-speaking part of Switzerland, who carried the marginalist approach furthest by describing the economic system in general mathematical terms. For each product, he said, there is a "demand function" that expresses the quantities of the product that consumers demand as dependent on its price, the prices of other related goods, the consumers' incomes, and their tastes. For each product there is also a "supply function" that expresses the quantities producers will supply dependent on their costs of production, the prices of productive services, and the level of technical knowledge. In the market, for each product there is a point of "equilibrium"—analogous to the equilibrium of forces in classical mechanics—at which a single price will satisfy both consumers and producers. It is not difficult to analyze the conditions under which equilibrium is possible for a single product. But equilibrium in one market depends on what happens in other markets (a "market" in this sense being not a place or location but a complex array of transactions involving a single good). This is true of every market. And because there are literally millions of markets in a modern economy, "general equilibrium" involves the simultaneous determination of partial equilibria in all markets.

Walras's efforts to describe the economy in this way led the Austro-American historian of economic thought Joseph Schumpeter to call Walras's work "the Magna Carta of economics." While undeniably abstract, Walrasian economics still provides an analytical framework for incorporating all the elements of a complete theory of the economic system. It is not too much to say that nearly the whole of modern economics is Walrasian economics, and modern theories of money, employment, international trade, and economic growth can be seen as Walrasian general equilibrium theories in a highly simplified form.

The years between the publication of Marshall's *Principles of Economics* (1890) and the stock market crash of 1929 may be described as years of reconciliation, consolidation, and refinement for the marginalists. The three schools of marginalist doctrines gradually coalesced into a single mainstream that became known as neoclassical economics. The theory of utility was reduced to an axiomatic system that could be applied to the analysis of consumer behaviour under almost any circumstance. The concept of marginalism in consumption led eventually to the idea of marginal productivity in production, and with it came a new theory of distribution in which wages, profits, interest, and rent were all shown to depend on the "marginal value product" of a factor. Marshall's concept of "external economies and diseconomies" (any external effects, either positive or negative, that a firm or entity might have on people, places, or other markets) was developed by his leading pupil at the University of Cambridge, Arthur Pigou, into a far-reaching distinction between private costs and social costs, thus establishing the basis of welfare theory as a separate branch of economic inquiry. This era also saw a gradual development of monetary theory (which explains how the level of all prices is determined as distinct from the determination of individual prices), notably by the Swedish economist Knut Wicksell. In the 1930s the growing harmony and unity of economics was rudely shattered, first by the simultaneous publication of the American economist Edward Chamberlin's *Theory of Monopolistic Competition* and the British economist Joan Robinson's *Economics of Imperfect Competition* in 1933, then by the appearance of the British economist John Maynard Keynes's *General Theory of Employment, Interest and Money* in 1936.

THE CRITICS

Before going on, it is necessary to take note of the rise and fall of the German historical school and the American institutionalist school, which leveled a steady barrage of critical attacks on the orthodox mainstream. The German historical economists, who had many different views, basically rejected the idea of an abstract economics with its supposedly universal laws: they urged the necessity of studying concrete facts in national contexts. While they gave impetus to the study of economic history, they failed to persuade their colleagues that their method was invariably superior.

The institutionalists are more difficult to categorize. Institutional economics, as the term is narrowly understood, refers to a movement in American economic thought associated with such names as Thorstein Veblen, Wesley C. Mitchell, and John R. Commons. These thinkers had little in common aside from their dissatisfaction with orthodox economics because of its tendency to cut itself off from the other social sciences, its preoccupation with the automatic market mechanism, and its abstract theorizing. Moreover, they failed to develop a unified theoretical apparatus that would replace or supplement the orthodox theory. This may explain why the phrase *institutional economics* has become little more than a synonym for *descriptive economics*. Particularly in the United States, institutional economics was the dominant style of economic thought during the period between World Wars I and II. At the time there was an expectation that institutional economics would furnish a new interdisciplinary social science. Although there is no longer an institutionalist movement in economics, the spirit of the old institutionalism lived on in such best-selling works as Canadian-born economist John Kenneth Galbraith's *The Affluent Society* (1969) and *The New Industrial State* (1967). In addition, there is the "new institutionalism" that links economic behaviour with societal concerns. This school is represented by such scholars as Oliver Williamson and Douglass North, who view institutions as conventions and norms that develop within a market economy to minimize the "transaction costs" of market activity.

It was through the innovations of the 1930s that the theory of monopolist, or imperfect, competition was integrated into neoclassical economics. Nineteenth-century economists had devoted their attention to two extreme types of market structure, either that of "pure monopoly" (in which a single seller controls the entire market for one product) or that of "pure competition" (meaning markets with many sellers, highly informed buyers, and a single, standard product). The theory of monopolistic competition recognized the range of market structures that lie between these extremes, including (1) markets having many sellers with "differentiated products," employing brand names, guarantees, and special packaging that cause consumers to regard the product of each seller as unique, (2) "oligopoly" markets, dominated by a few large firms, and (3) "monopsony" markets, with many sellers but a single monopolistic buyer. The theory produced the powerful conclusion that competitive industries, in which each seller has a partial monopoly because of product differentiation, will tend to have an excessive number of firms, all charging a higher price than they would if the industry were perfectly competitive. Since product differentiation—and the associated phenomenon of advertising—seems to be characteristic of most industries in developed capitalist economies, the new theory was immediately hailed as injecting a healthy dose of realism into orthodox price theory. Unfortunately, its scope was limited, and it failed to provide a satisfactory explanation of price determination under conditions of oligopoly. This was a significant omission, because in advanced economies most manufacturing and even most service industries are dominated by a few large firms. The resulting gap at the centre of modern price theory shows that economists cannot fully explain the conditions under which multi-national firms conduct their affairs.

KEYNESIAN ECONOMICS

The second major breakthrough of the 1930s, the theory of income determination, stemmed primarily from the work of John Maynard Keynes, who asked questions that in some sense had never been posed before. Keynes was interested in the level of national income and the volume of employment rather than in the equilibrium of the firm or the allocation of resources. He was still concerned with the problem of demand and supply, but "demand" in the Keynesian model means the total level of effective demand in the economy, while "supply" means the country's capacity to produce. When effective demand falls short of productive capacity, the result is unemployment and depression; conversely, when demand exceeds the capacity to produce, the result is inflation.

Central to Keynesian economics is an analysis of the determinants of effective demand. The Keynesian model of effective demand consists essentially of three spending streams: consumption expenditures, invest-ment expenditures, and government expenditures, each of which is independently determined. (Foreign trade is ignored.) Keynes attempted to show that the level of effective demand, as determined in this model, may well exceed or fall short of the physical capacity to pro-duce goods and services. He also proved that there is no automatic tendency to produce at a level that results in the full employment of all available human capital and equipment. His findings reversed the assumption that economic systems would automatically tend toward full employment.

John Maynard Keynes in his study. Walter Stoneman/Hulton Archive/Getty Images

By remaining focused on macroeconomic aggregates (such as total consumption and total investment) and by deliberately simplifying the relationships between these economic variables, Keynes achieved a powerful model that could be applied to a wide range of practical problems. Others subsequently refined his system of analysis (some have said that Keynes himself would hardly have recognized it), and it became thoroughly assimilated into established economic theory. Still, it is not too much to say that Keynes was perhaps the first economist to have added something truly new to economics since Walras put forth his equilibrium theory in the 1870s.

Keynesian economics as conceived by Keynes was entirely "static"; that is, it did not involve time as an important variable. But one of Keynes's adherents, Roy Harrod, emphasized the importance of time in his simple macroeconomic model of a growing economy. With the publication of *Towards a Dynamic Economics* (1948), Harrod launched an entirely new specialty, "growth theory," which soon absorbed the attention of an increasing number of economists.

DEVELOPMENTS AFTER WORLD WAR II

The 25-year period following World War II can be viewed as an era in which the nature of economics as a discipline was transformed. First of all, mathematics came to permeate virtually every branch of the field. As economists moved from a limited use of differential and integral calculus, matrix algebra represented an attempt to add a quantitative dimension to a general equilibrium model of the economy. Matrix algebra was also associated with the advent of input-output analysis, an empirical method of reducing the technical relations between industries to a manageable system of simultaneous equations. A closely related phenomenon was the development of linear programming and activity analysis, which opened up the possibility of applying numerical solutions to industrial problems. This advance also introduced economists to the mathematics of inequalities (as opposed to exact equation). Likewise, the emergence of growth economics promoted the use of difference and differential equations.

The wider application of mathematical economics was joined by an increasing sophistication of empirical work under the rubric of "econometrics," a field comprising economic theory, mathematical model building, and statistical testing of economic predictions. The development of econometrics had an impact on economics in general, since those who formulated new theories began to cast them in terms that allowed empirical testing.

New developments in economics were not limited to methodological approaches. Interest in the less-developed countries returned in the later decades of the 20th century, especially as economists recognized their long neglect of Adam Smith's "inquiry into the causes of the wealth of nations." There was also a conviction that economic planning was needed to lessen the gap between the rich and poor countries. Out of these concerns came the field of development economics, with offshoots in regional economics, urban economics, and environmental economics.

These postwar developments were best exemplified not by the emergence of new techniques or by additions to the economics curriculum but by the disappearance of divisive "schools," by the increasingly standardized professional training of economists throughout the world, and by the transformation of the science from a rarefied academic exercise into an operational discipline geared to practical advice. This transformation brought prestige (the Nobel Prize in Economic Sciences was first awarded in 1969) but also new responsibility to the profession: now that economics really mattered, economists had to reconcile the differences that so often exist between analytical precision and economic relevance.

RADICAL CRITIQUES

The question of relevance was at the centre of a "radical critique" of economics that developed along with the student revolts and social movements of the late 1960s. The radical critics declared that economics had become a defense of the status quo and that its practitioners had joined the power elite. The marginal techniques of the

ECONOMETRICS

Econometrics is the statistical and mathematical analysis of economic relationships. Econometricians create equations to describe phenomena such as the relationship between changes in price and demand. They also estimate production functions and cost functions for firms, supply-and-demand functions for industries, income distribution in an economy, macroeconomic models and models of the monetary sector for policy makers, and business cycles and growth for forecasting. Information derived from these models helps both private businesses and governments make decisions and set monetary and fiscal policy.

economists, ran the argument, were profoundly conservative in their bias, because they encouraged a piecemeal rather than a revolutionary approach to social problems. Likewise, the tendency in theoretical work to ignore the everyday context of economic activity amounted in practice to the tacit acceptance of prevailing institutions. The critics said that economics should abandon its claim of being a value-free social science and address itself to the great questions of the day—those of civil rights, poverty, imperialism, and environmental pollution—even at the cost of analytical rigour and theoretical elegance.

It is true that the study of economics encourages a belief in reform rather than revolution—yet it must be understood that this is so because economics as a science does not provide enough certitude for any thorough-going reconstruction of the social order. It is also true that most economists tend to be deeply suspicious of monopoly in all forms, including state monopolies, and for this reason they tend to favour competition between independent producers as a way of diffusing economic power. Finally, most economists prefer to be silent on large questions if they have nothing to offer beyond the expression of personal preferences. Their greater concern lies in the professional standards of their discipline, and this may mean in some cases frankly conceding that economics has as yet nothing very interesting to say about the larger social questions.

METHODS OF ECONOMICS

Economists, like other social scientists, are sometimes confronted with the charge that their discipline is not a science. Human behaviour, it is said, cannot be analyzed with the same objectivity as the behaviour of atoms and molecules. Value judgments, philosophical preconceptions, and ideological biases unavoidably interfere with the attempt to derive conclusions that are independent of the particular economist espousing them. Moreover, there is no realistic laboratory in which economists can test their hypotheses.

In response, economists are wont to distinguish between "positive economics" and "normative economics." Positive economics seeks to establish facts: If butter producers are paid a subsidy, will the price of butter be lowered? Will a rise in wages in the automotive industry reduce the employment of automobile workers? Will the devaluation of currency improve a country's balance of payments? Does monopoly foster technical progress? Normative economics, on the other hand, is concerned not with matters of fact but with questions of policy or of trade-offs between "good" and "bad" effects: Should the goal of price stability be sacrificed to that of full employment? Should income be taxed at a progressive rate? Should there be legislation in favour of competition?

Because positive economics in principle involves no judgments of value, its findings may appear impersonal. This is not to deny that most of the interesting economic

An American auto worker. Scott Olson/Getty Images

propositions involve the addition of definite value judgments to a body of established facts, that ideological bias creeps into the very selection of the questions that economists investigate, or even that much practical economic advice is loaded with concealed value judgments (the better to persuade rather than merely to advise). This is only to say that economists are human. Their commitment to the ideal of value-free positive economics (or to the candid declaration of personal values in normative economics) serves as a defense against the attempts of special interests to bend the science to their own purposes. The best assurance against bias on the part of any particular economist comes from the criticism of other economists. The best protection against special pleading in the name of science is founded in the professional standards of scientists.

METHODS OF INFERENCE

If the science of economics is not based on laboratory experiments (as are the "hard" sciences), then how are facts established? Simply put, facts are established by means of statistical inference. Economists typically begin by describing the terms they believe to be most important in the area under study. Then they construct a "model" of the real world, deliberately repressing some of its features and emphasizing others. Using this model, they abstract, isolate, and simplify, thus imposing a certain order on a theoretical world. They then manipulate the model by a process of logical deduction, arriving eventually at some prediction or implication that is of general significance. At this point, they compare their findings to the real world to see if the prediction is borne out by observed events.

But these observable events are merely a sample, and they may fail to represent real-world examples. This raises a central problem of statistical inference: namely, what can be construed about a population from a sample of the population? Statistical inference may serve as an agreed-upon procedure for making such judgments, but it cannot remove all elements of doubt. Thus the empirical truths of economics are invariably surrounded by a band of uncertainty, and economists therefore make assertions that are "probable" or "likely," or they state propositions with "a certain degree of confidence" because it is unlikely that their findings could have come about by chance.

It follows that judgments are at the heart of both positive and normative economics. It is easy to see, however, that judgments about "degrees of confidence" and "statistical levels of significance" are of a totally different order from those that crop up in normative economics. Normative statements—that individuals should be allowed to spend income as they choose, that people should not be free to control material resources and to employ others, or that governments must offer relief for the victims of economic distress—represent the kind of value judgments associated with the act of disguising personal preferences as scientific conclusions. There is no room for such value judgments in positive economics.

TESTING THEORIES

Most assumptions in economic theory cannot be tested directly. For example, there is the famous assumption of price theory that entrepreneurs strive to maximize profits. Attempts to find out whether they do, by asking them, usually fail; after all, entrepreneurs are no more fully conscious of their own motives than other people are. A logical approach would be to observe entrepreneurs in action. But that would require knowing what sort of action is associated with profit maximizing, which is to say that one would have drawn out all the implications of a profit-maximizing model. Thus one would be testing an assumption about business behaviour by comparing the predictions of a theory of the firm with observations from the real world.

This is not as easy as it sounds. Since the predictions of economics are couched in the nature of probability statements, there can be no such thing as a conclusive, once-and-for-all test of an economic hypothesis. The science of statistics cannot prove any hypothesis; it can only fail to disprove it. Hence economic theories tend to survive until they are falsified repeatedly with new or better data. This is not because they are economic theories but because the attempt to compare predictions with outcomes in the social sciences is always limited by the rules of statistical inference.

It is not remarkable that competing theories exist to explain the same phenomena, with economists disagreeing as to which theory is to be preferred. Much has been written about the uncertain accuracy of economists' predictions. While economists can foretell the effects of specific changes in the economy, they are better at predicting the direction rather than the actual magnitude of events. When economists predict that a tax cut will raise national income, one may be confident that the prediction is accurate; when they predict that it will raise national income by a certain amount in three years, however, the forecast is likely to miss the mark. The reason is that most economic models do not contain any explicit reference to the passage of time and hence have little to say about how long it takes for a certain effect to make itself felt. Short-period predictions generally fare better than long-period ones. Since its development in the 1990s, experimental economics has, in fact, been testing economic hypotheses in artificial situations—often by using monetary rewards and student subjects. Much of this innovative work has been stimulated by the ascendance of game theory, the mathematical analysis of strategic interactions between economic agents, represented in such works as *Theory of Games and Economic Behaviour* (1944) by John von Neumann and Oskar Morgenstern. Aspects of game theory have since been applied to nearly every subfield in economics, and its influence has been felt not just in economics but in sociology, political science, and, above all, biology. Because game theory fosters the construction of experimental game situations, it has helped diminish the old accusation that economics is not a laboratory-based discipline.

MICROECONOMICS

Since Keynes, economic theory has been of two kinds: macroeconomics, or the study of the determinants of national income, and traditional microeconomics, which approaches the economy as if it were made up only of business firms and households (ignoring governments, banks, charities, trade unions, and all other economic institutions) interacting in two kinds of markets—product markets and those for productive services, or factor markets. Households appear as buyers in product markets and as sellers in factor markets, where they offer human labour, machines, and land for sale or hire. Firms appear as sellers in product markets and as buyers in factor markets. In each type of market, price is determined by the interaction of demand and supply. The task of microeconomic theory is to say something meaningful about the forces that shape demand and supply.

THEORY OF CHOICE

Firms face certain technical constraints in producing goods and services, and households have definite preferences for some products over others. It is possible to express the technical constraints facing business firms through a series of production functions, one for each firm. A production function is simply an equation that expresses the fact that a firm's output depends on the quantity of inputs it employs and, in particular, that inputs can be technically combined in different proportions to produce a given level of output. For example, a production engineer could calculate the largest possible output that could be produced with every possible combination of inputs. This calculation would define the range of production possibilities open to a firm, but it cannot predict how much the firm will produce, what mixture of products it will make, or what combination of inputs it will adopt; these depend on the prices of products and the prices of inputs (factors of production), which have yet to be determined. If the firm wants to maximize profits (defined as the difference between the sales value of its output and the cost of its inputs), it will select that combination of inputs that minimizes its expenses and therefore maximizes its revenue. Firms can seek efficiencies through the production function, but production choices depend, in part, on the demand for products. This leads to the part played by households in the system.

Each household is endowed with definite "tastes" that can be expressed in a series of "utility functions." A utility function (an equation similar to the production function) shows that the pleasure or satisfaction households derive from consumption will depend on the products they purchase and on how they consume these products. Utility functions provide a general description of the household's preferences between all the paired alternatives it might confront. Here, too, it is necessary to assume that households seek to maximize satisfaction and that they will distribute their given incomes among available consumer goods in a way that derives the largest possible "utility" from consumption. Their incomes, however, remain to be determined.

In economic theory, the production function contributes to the calculation of supply curves (graphic representations of the relationship between product price and quantity that a seller is willing and able to supply) for firms in product markets and demand curves (graphic representations of the relationship between product price and the quantity of the product demanded) for firms in factor markets. Similarly, the utility function contributes to the calculation of demand curves for households in product markets and the supply curves for households in factor markets. All of these demand and supply curves express the quantities demanded and supplied as a function of prices not because price alone determines economic behaviour but because the purpose is to arrive at a theory of price determination. Much of microeconomic theory is devoted to showing how various production and utility functions, coupled with certain assumptions about behaviour, lead to demand and supply curves such as those depicted in the figure.

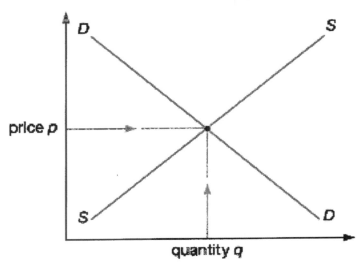

price p

quantity q

© 2003 Encyclopædia Britannica, Inc.

Illustration of the relationship of price to supply (S) and demand (D).

Not all demand and supply curves look alike. The essential point, however, is that most demand curves are negatively inclined (consumers demand less as the price rises), while most supply curves are positively inclined (suppliers are likely to produce more at higher prices). The participants in a market will be driven to the price at which the two curves intersect; this price is called the "equilibrium" price or "market-clearing" price because it is the only price at which supply and demand are equal.

For example, in a market for butter, any change—in the production function of dairy farmers, in the utility function of butter consumers, in the prices of cows, grassland, and milking equipment, in the incomes of butter consumers, or in the prices of nondairy products that consumers buy—can be shown to lead to definite changes in the equilibrium price of butter and in the equilibrium quantity of butter produced. Even more predictable are the effects of government-imposed price limits, taxes on butter producers, or price-support programs for dairy farmers, which can be forecast with reasonable certainty. As a rule, the prediction will refer only to the direction of change (the price will go up or down), but if the demand and supply curves of butter can be defined in quantitative terms, one may also be able to foresee the actual magnitude of the change.

THEORY OF ALLOCATION

The analysis of the behaviour of firms and households is to some extent symmetrical: all economic agents are conceived of as ordering a series of attainable positions in terms of an entity they are trying to maximize. A firm aims to maximize its use of input combinations, while a household attempts to maximize product combinations. From the maximizing point of view, some combinations are better than others, and the best combination is called the "optimal" or "efficient" combination. As a rule, the optimal allocation equalizes the returns of the marginal (or last) unit to be transferred between all the possible uses. In the theory of the firm, an optimum allocation of outlays among the factors is the same for all factors; the "law of eventually diminishing marginal utility," a property of a wide range of utility functions, ensures that such an optimum exists. These are merely particular examples of the "equimarginal principle," a tool that can be applied to any decision that involves alternative courses of action. Not only is it at the core of the theory of the firm and the theory of consumer behaviour, but it also underlies the theory of money, of capital, and of international trade. In fact, the whole of microeconomics is nothing more than the spelling out of this principle in ever-wider contexts.

The equimarginal principle can be widely applied because economics furnishes a technique for thinking about decisions, regardless of their character and who makes them. Military planners, for example, may consider a variety of weapons in the light of a single objective, damaging an enemy. Some of the weapons are effective against the enemy's army, some against the enemy's navy, and some against the air force; the problem is to find an optimal allocation of the defense budget, one that equalizes the marginal contribution of each type of weapon. But defense departments rarely have a single objective; along with maximizing damage to an enemy, there may be another objective, such as minimizing losses from attacks. In that case, the equimarginal principle will not suffice; it is necessary to know how the department ranks the two objectives in order of importance. The ranking of objectives can be determined through a utility function or a preference function.

When an institution pursues multiple ends, decisions about how to achieve them require a weighting of the ends. Every decision involves a "production function"— a statement of what is technically feasible—and a "utility function." The equimarginal principle is then invoked to provide an efficient, optimal strategy. This principle applies just as well to the running of hospitals, churches, and schools as to the conduct of a business enterprise and is as applicable to the location of an international airport as it is to the design of a development plan for a country. This is why economists advise on activities that are obviously not being conducted for economic reasons.

The general application of economics in unfamiliar places is associated with American economist Gary Becker, whose work has been characterized as "economics imperialism" for influencing areas beyond the boundaries of the discipline's traditional concerns. In such books as *An Economic Approach to Human Behavior* (1976) and *A Treatise on the Family* (1981), Becker, who won the Nobel Prize in Economic Sciences in 1992, made innovative applications of "rational choice theory." His work in rational choice, which went outside established economic practices to incorporate social phenomena, applied the principle of utility maximization to all decision making and appropriated the notion of determinate equilibrium outcomes to evaluate such noneconomic phenomena as marriage, divorce, the decision to have children, and choices about children's education.

MACROECONOMICS

As stated earlier, macroeconomics is concerned with the aggregate outcome of individual actions. Keynes's "consumption function," for example, which relates aggregate consumption to national income, is not built up from individual consumer behaviour; it is simply an empirical generalization. The focus is on income and expenditure flows rather than on the operation of markets. Purchasing power flows through the system— from business investment to consumption—but it flows out of the system in two ways, in the form of personal and business savings. Counterbalancing the savings are investment expenditures, however, in the form of new capital goods, production plants, houses, and so forth. These constitute new injections of purchasing power in every period. Since savings and investments are carried out by different people for different motives, there is no reason why "leakages" and "injections" should be equal in every period. If they are not equal, national income (the sum of all income payments to the factors of production) will rise or fall in the next period. When planned savings equal planned investment, income will be at an equilibrium level, but when the plans of savers do not match those of investors, the level of income will go on changing until the two do match.

This simple model can take on increasingly complex dimensions by making investment a function of the interest rate or by introducing other variables such as the government budget, the money market, labour markets, imports and exports, or foreign investment. But all this is far removed from the problem of resource allocation and from the maximizing behaviour of individual economic agents, the traditional microeconomic concerns.

The split between macroeconomics and microeconomics—a difference in questions asked and in the style of answers obtained—has continued since the Keynesian revolution in the 1930s. Macroeconomic theory, however, has undergone significant change. The Keynesian system was amplified in the 1950s by the introduction of the Phillips curve, which established an inverse relationship between wage-price inflation and unemployment. At first, this relationship seemed to be so firmly founded as to constitute a virtual "law" in economics. Gradually, however, adverse evidence about the Phillips curve appeared, and in 1968 *The Role of Monetary Policy*, first delivered as Milton Friedman's presidential address to the American Economic Association, introduced the notorious concept of "the natural rate of unemployment" (the minimum rate of unemployment that will prevent businesses from continually raising prices). Friedman's paper defined the essence of the school of economic thought now known as monetarism and marked the end of the Keynesian revolution, because it implied that the full-employment policies of Keynesianism would only succeed in sparking inflation. American economist Robert Lucas carried monetarism one step further: if economic agents were perfectly rational, they would correctly anticipate any effort on the part of governments to increase aggregate demand and adjust their behaviour. This concept of "rational expectations" means that macroeconomic policy measures are ineffective not only in the long run but in the very short run. It was Lucas's concept of "rational expectations" that marked the nadir of Keynesianism, and macroeconomics after the 1970s was never again the consensual corpus of ideas it had been before.

NEOCLASSICAL ECONOMICS

The preceding portrait of microeconomics and macroeconomics is characteristic of the elementary orthodox economics offered in undergraduate courses in the West, often under the heading "neoclassical economics." Given its name by Thorstein Veblen at the turn of the 20th century, this approach emphasizes the way in which firms and individuals maximize their objectives. Only at the graduate level do students encounter the many important economic problems and aspects of economic behaviour that are not caught in the neoclassical net. For example, economics is, first and foremost, the study of competition,

MONETARISM

Monetarism is the school of economic thought that maintains that the money supply (the total amount of money in an economy, in the form of coin, currency, and bank deposits) is the chief determinant on the demand side of short-run economic activity. The American economist Milton Friedman was generally regarded as monetarism's leading exponent. Friedman and other monetarists advocated a macroeconomic theory and policy that diverge significantly from those of the formerly dominant Keynesian school. The monetarist approach became influential during the 1970s and early '80s.

Underlying the monetarist theory is the equation of exchange, which is expressed as $MV = PQ$. Here M is the supply of money, and V is the velocity of turnover of money (i.e., the number of times per year that the average dollar in the money supply is spent for goods and services), while P is the average price level at which each of the goods and services is sold, and Q represents the quantity of goods and services produced.

The monetarists believe that the direction of causation is from left to right in the equation; that is, as the money supply increases with a constant and predictable V, one can expect an increase in either P or Q. An increase in Q means that P will remain relatively constant, while an increase in P will occur if there is no corresponding increase in the quantity of goods and services produced. In short, a change in the money supply directly affects and determines production, employment, and price levels. The effects of changes in the money supply, however, become manifest only after a significant period of time.

Friedman contended that the government should seek to promote economic stability, but only by

Milton Friedman. George Rose/Getty Images

controlling the rate of growth of the money supply. It could achieve this by following a simple rule that stipulates that the money supply be increased at a constant annual rate tied to the potential growth of gross domestic product (GDP) and expressed as a percentage (e.g., an increase from 3 to 5 percent). Monetarism thus posited that the steady, moderate growth of the money supply could in many cases ensure a steady rate of economic growth with low inflation.

Monetarism's linking of economic growth with rates of increase of the money supply was proved incorrect, however, by changes in the U.S. economy during the 1980s. First, new and hybrid types of bank deposits obscured the kinds of savings that had traditionally been used by economists to calculate the money supply. Second, a decline in the rate of inflation caused people to spend less, which thereby decreased velocity (V). These changes diminished the ability to predict the effects of money growth on growth of nominal GDP.

but neoclassical economics focuses almost exclusively on one kind of competition—price competition. This focus fails to consider other competitive approaches, such as quantity competition (evidenced by discount stores, such as the American merchandising giant Wal-Mart, that use economies of scale to pass cost savings onto consumers) and quality competition (seen in product innovations and other forms of nonprice competition such as convenient location, better servicing, and faster deliveries). Advertising also plays an important role in the process of competition—in fact, it may be more significant than the competitive strategies of raising or lowering prices, yet standard neoclassical economics has little to say about advertising. The neoclassical approach also tends to ignore the complex nature of business enterprises and the organizational structures that guide effective production. In short, neoclassical economics makes important points about pricing and competition, but in its strictest definition it is not equipped to deal with the varied economic problems of the modern world.

FIELDS OF ECONOMICS

The principal fields of contemporary economics include money, economic growth, development economics, public finance, international economics, labour, industrial organization, agriculture, law and economics, information economics, and financial economics.

MONEY

One of the oldest, most widely accepted functions of government is control over money, the basic medium of exchange. The dramatic effects of changes in the quantity of money on the level of prices and the volume of economic activity were recognized and thoroughly analyzed in the 18th century. In the 19th century there developed a tradition known as the "quantity theory of money," which held that any change in the supply of money can only be absorbed by variations in the general level of prices (the purchasing power of money). In consequence, prices will tend to change proportionately with the quantity of money in circulation. Simply put, the quantity theory of money stated that inflation or deflation could be controlled by varying the quantity of money in circulation inversely with the level of prices.

One of the targets of Keynes's attack on traditional thinking in his *General Theory of Employment, Interest*

The gold vault in the Federal Reserve Bank of New York. ©
National Geographic/SuperStock

and Money (1935–36) was this quantity theory of money. Keynes asserted that the link between the money stock and the level of national income was weak and that the effect of the money supply on prices was virtually nil—at least in economies with heavy unemployment, such as those of the 1930s. He emphasized instead the importance of government budgetary and tax policy and direct control of investment. As a consequence of Keynes's theory, economists came to regard monetary policy as more or less ineffective in controlling the volume of economic activity.

In the 1960s, however, there was a remarkable revival of the older view, at least among a small but growing school of American monetary economists led by Friedman. They argued that the effects of fiscal policy are unreliable unless the quantity of money is regulated at the same time. Basing their work on the old quantity theory of money, they tested the new version on a variety of data for different countries and time periods. They concluded that the quantity of money does matter. *A Monetary History of the United States, 1867–1960*, by Milton Friedman and Anna Schwartz (1963), which became the benchmark work of monetarism, criticized Keynesian fiscal measures along with all other attempts at fine-tuning the economy. With its emphasis on money supply, monetarism enjoyed an enormous vogue in the 1970s but faded by the 1990s as economists increasingly adopted an approach that combined the old Keynesian emphasis on fiscal policy with a new understanding of monetary policy.

GROWTH AND DEVELOPMENT

The study of economic growth and development is not a single branch of economics but falls, in fact, into two quite different fields. The two fields—growth and development—employ different methods of analysis and address two distinct types of inquiry.

Development economics is easy to characterize as one of the three major subfields of economics, along with microeconomics and macroeconomics. More specifically, development economics resembles economic history in that it seeks to explain the changes that occur in economic systems over time.

The subject of economic growth is not so easy to characterize. Indeed, it is the most technically demanding field in the whole of modern economics, impossible to grasp for anyone who lacks a command of differential calculus. Its focus is the properties of equilibrium paths, rather than equilibrium states. In applying economic growth theory, one makes a model of the economy and puts it into motion, requiring that the time paths described by the variables be self-sustaining in the sense that they continue to be related to each other in certain characteristic ways. Then one can investigate the way economics might approach and reach these steady-state growth paths from given starting points. Beautiful and frequently surprising theorems have emerged from this experience, but as yet there are no really testable implications nor even definite insights into how economies grow.

Growth theory began with the investigations by Roy Harrod in England and Evsey Domar in the United States. Their independent work, joined in the Harrod-Domar model, is based on natural rates of growth and warranted rates of growth. Keynes had shown that new investment has a multiplier effect on income and that the increased income generates extra savings to match the extra investment, without which the higher income level could not be sustained. One may think of this as being repeated from period to period, remembering that investment, apart from raising income disproportionately, also generates the capacity to produce more output. This results in products that cannot be sold unless there is more demand—that is, more consumption and more investment. This is all there is to the model. It contains one behavioral condition: that people tend to save a certain proportion of extra income, a tendency that can be measured. It also contains one technical condition: that investment generates additional output, a fact that can be established. And it contains one equilibrium condition:

that planned saving must equal planned investment in every period if the income level of the period is to be sustained. Given these three conditions, the model generates a time path of income and even indicates what will happen if income falls off the path.

More complex models have since been built, incorporating different saving ratios for different groups in the population, technical conditions for each industry, definite assumptions about the character of technical progress in the economy, monetary and financial equations, and much more. The new growth theory of the 1990s was labeled "endogenous growth theory" because it attempted to explain technical change as the result of profit-motivated research and development (R&D) expenditure by private firms. This was driven by competition along the lines of what Joseph Schumpeter called product innovations (as distinct from process innovations). In contrast to the Harrod-Domar model, which viewed growth as exogenous, or coming from outside variables, the endogenous theory emphasizes growth from within the system. This approach enjoyed, and still enjoys, an enormous vogue, partly because it seemed to offer governments a new means of promoting economic growth—namely, national innovation policies designed to stimulate more private and public R&D spending.

PUBLIC FINANCE

Taxation has been a concern of economists since the time of David Ricardo. Much interest centres on determining who really pays a tax. If a corporation faced with a profits tax reacts by raising the prices it charges for goods and services, it might succeed in passing the tax on to the consumer. If, however, sales decline as a result of the rise in price, the firm may have to reduce production and lay off some of its workers, meaning that the tax burden has been passed along not only to consumers but to wage earners and shareholders as well.

This simple example shows how complex the so-called "tax incidence" may be. The literature of public finance in the 19th century was devoted to such problems, but Keynesian economics replaced the older emphasis on tax incidence with the analysis of the impact of government expenditures on the level of income and employment. It was some time, however, before economists realized that they lacked a theory of government expenditures—that is, a set of criteria for determining what activities should be supported by governments and what the relative expenditure on

The debate over taxation gave rise, in part, to the Tea Party and Occupy Wall Street political movements. Darren McCollester/ Getty Images

each should be. The field of public finance has since attempted to devise such criteria. Decisions on public expenditures have proved to be susceptible to much of the traditional analysis of microeconomics. New developments in the 1960s expanded on a technique known as cost-benefit analysis, which tries to appraise all of the economic costs and benefits, direct and indirect, of a particular activity so as to decide how to distribute a given public budget most effectively between different activities. This technique, first put forth by Jules Dupuit in the 19th century, has been applied to everything from the construction of hydroelectric dams to the control of tuberculosis. Its exponents hoped that the same type of analysis that had proved so fruitful in the past in analyzing individual choice would also succeed with problems of social choice.

Building upon 18th- and 19th-century mathematical studies of the voting process, the Scottish economist Duncan Black brought a political dimension to cost-benefit studies. His book *The Theory of Committees and Elections* (1958) became the basis of public choice theory. As expressed in the book *Calculus of Consent* (1962) by the American economists James Buchanan and Gordon Tullock, public choice theory applies the cost-benefit analysis seen in private decision making to political decision making. Politicians are conceived of as maximizing electoral votes in the same way that firms seek to maximize profits, while political parties are conceived of as organizing electoral support in the same way that firms organize themselves as cartels or power blocs to lobby governments on their behalf. Public choice challenged the notion, implicit in early public finance theory, that politicians always identify their own interest with that of the country as a whole.

INTERNATIONAL ECONOMICS

Ever since 19th-century economists put forth their theories of international economics, the subject has consisted of two distinct but connected parts: (1) the "pure theory of international trade," which seeks to account for the gains obtained from trade and to explain how these gains are distributed among countries, and (2) the "theory of balance-of-payments adjustments," which analyzes the workings of the foreign exchange market, the effects of alterations in the exchange rate of a currency, and the relations between the balance of payments and level of economic activity.

In modern times, the Ricardian pure theory of international trade was reformulated by the American economist Paul Samuelson, improving on the earlier work of two Swedish economists, Eli Heckscher and Bertil Ohlin. The so-called Heckscher-Ohlin theory explains the pattern of international trade as determined by the relative land, labour, and capital endowments of countries: a country will tend to have a relative cost advantage when producing goods that maximize the use of its relatively abundant factors of production (thus countries with cheap labour are best suited to export products that require significant amounts of labour). This theory subsumes Ricardo's law of comparative costs but goes beyond it in linking the pattern of trade to the economic structure of trading nations. It implies that foreign trade is a substitute for international movements of labour and capital, which raises the intriguing question of whether foreign trade may work to equalize the prices of all factors of production in all trading countries. Whatever the answer, the Heckscher-Ohlin theory provides a model for analyzing the effects of a change in trade on the industrial structures of economies and, in particular, on the distribution of income between factors of production.

One early study of the Heckscher-Ohlin theory was carried out by Wassily Leontief, a Russian American economist. Leontief observed that the United States was relatively rich with capital. According to the theory, therefore, the United States should have been exporting capital-intensive goods while importing labour-intensive goods. His finding, that U.S. exports were relatively more labour-intensive and imports more capital intensive, became known as the Leontief Paradox because it disputed the Heckscher-Ohlin theory. Recent efforts in international economics have attempted to refine the Heckscher-Ohlin model and test it on a wider range of empirical evidence.

LABOUR

Like monetary and international economics, labour economics is an old economic speciality. Its raison d'être comes from the peculiarities of labour as a commodity. Unlike land or machinery, labour itself is not bought and sold; rather, its services are hired and rented out. But since people cannot be disassociated from their services, various nonmonetary considerations play a concealed role in the sale of labour services.

For many years labour economics was concerned solely with the demand side of the labour market. This one-sided view held that wages were determined by the "marginal productivity of labour"—that is, by the

Wal-Mart is the largest private employer in the world and has been criticized for actively discouraging unionization among its employees. Chris Hondros/Getty Images

relationships of production and by consumer demand. If the supply of labour came into the picture at all, it was merely to allow for the presence of trade unions. Unions, it was believed, could only raise wages by limiting the supply of labour. Later in the 20th century, the supply side of the labour market attracted the attention of economists, which shifted from the individual worker to the household as a supplier of labour services. The increasing number of married women entering the labour force and the wide disparities and fluctuations observed in the rate that females participate in a labour force drew attention to the fact that an individual's decision to supply labour is strongly related to the size, age structure, and asset holdings of the household to which he or she belongs.

Next, the concept of human capital—that people make capital investments in their children and in themselves in the form of education and training, that they seek better job opportunities, and that they are willing to migrate to other labour markets—has served as a unifying explanation of the diverse activities of households in labour markets. Capital theory has since become the dominant analytical tool of the labour economists, replacing or supplementing the traditional theory of consumer behaviour. The economics of training and education, the economics of information, the economics of migration, the economics of health, and the economics of poverty are some of the by-products of this new perspective. A field that was at one time regarded as rather cut-and-dried has taken on new vitality.

Labour economics, old or new, has always regarded the explanation of wages as its principal task, including the factors determining the general level of wages in an economy and the reasons for wage differentials between industries and occupations. There is no question that wages are influenced by trade unions, and the impact of union activities is of increased importance at a time when governments are concerned with unemployment statistics. Questions of whether prices are being pushed up by the labour unions ("cost push") or pulled up by excess purchasing power ("demand pull") have become the issues in the larger debate on inflation—a controversy that is directly related to the debates in monetary economics mentioned earlier.

INDUSTRIAL ORGANIZATION

The principal concerns of industrial organization are the structure of markets, public policy toward monopoly, the regulation of public utilities, and the economics of technical change. The monopoly problem, or, more precisely, the problem of the maintenance of competition, does not fit well into the received body of economic thought. Economics started out, after all, as the theory of competitive enterprise, and even today its most impressive theorems require the assumption of numerous small firms, each having a negligible influence on price. Yet, as noted earlier, contemporary market structures tend toward oligopoly—competition among the few—with some industries dominated by firms so large their annual sales volume exceeds the national income of the smaller European countries. It is tempting to conclude that oligopoly is deleterious to economic welfare on the ground that it leads to the misallocation of resources. But some economists, notably Schumpeter, have argued that economic growth and technical progress are achieved not through free competition but by the enlargement of firms and the destruction of competition. According to this view, the giant firms compete not in price but in successful innovation, and this kind of competition has proved more effective for economic progress than the more traditional price competition.

This thesis makes somewhat less compelling the merits of "trust busting," largely taken for granted since the administration of U.S. Pres. Theodore Roosevelt first set about curbing the concentration of corporate power in the early 20th century. Instead, it points the way for a consideration of competition that seeks to attain the greatest benefit for society. For example, if four or five large firms in an oligopolistic industry compete on the basis of product quality, research, technology, or merchandising, the performance of the entire industry may well be more satisfactory than if it were reorganized into a price-competitive industry. But if the four or five giants compete only in sales promotion techniques, the outcome will likely be less favourable for society. One cannot, therefore, draw facile conclusions about the competitive results of different market structures.

Much uncertainty in the economic discussion of policies toward big business stems from the lack of a general theory of oligopoly. Perhaps a loose criterion for judging the desirability of different market structures is

ANTITRUST LAW

Antitrust law encompasses any legal restriction on business practices considered unfair or monopolistic. The United States has the longest standing policy of maintaining competition among business enterprises through a variety of laws. The best known is the Sherman Antitrust Act of 1890, which declared illegal "every contract, combination . . . or conspiracy in restraint of trade or commerce." Another important U.S. antitrust law, the Clayton Antitrust Act of 1914, as amended in 1936 by the Robinson–Patman Act, prohibits discrimination among customers through prices or other means; it also prohibits mergers of firms, or acquisitions of one firm by another, whenever the effect may be "to substantially lessen competition."

In Europe, antitrust legislation received much attention after World War II, when provisions against restraint of competition were embodied in a number of national laws and international agreements. The Commission of the European Union (EU) in Brussels regularly passes upon cases involving practices of companies trading in the EU. Its decisions are based upon Articles 85 and 86 of the Treaty of Rome (1957), which deal with rules of fair competition.

American economist William Baumol's concept of "contestable markets": if a market is easy to enter and to exit, it is "contestable" and hence workably competitive.

AGRICULTURE

Farming has long provided economists with their favourite example of a perfectly competitive industry. However, given the level of government regulation of and support for agriculture in most countries, farming also provides striking examples of the effects of price controls, income supports, output ceilings, and marketing cartels. Not surprisingly, agricultural economics commands attention wherever governments wish to stimulate farming or to protect farmers—which is to say everywhere.

Agricultural economists generally have been closer to their subject matter than other economists. In consequence, more is known about the technology of agriculture, the nature of farming costs, and the demand for agricultural goods than is known about any other industry. Thus the field of agricultural economics offers a rich literature on the basics of economic study, such as estimating a production function or plotting a demand curve.

LAW AND ECONOMICS

Among relatively new developments, one of the most remarkable is the growth of a discipline combining legal and economic concerns. Its origins in the 1970s are almost wholly due to the unintended effects of two articles by Ronald Coase, a British economist specializing in industrial organization. Before emigrating to the United States in 1950, Coase published *The Nature*

Indonesian farmers protest the government's market intervention in their business. Farmers are affected by market controls more than most other industries. AFP/Getty Images

of the Firm (1937), which was the first paper to pose a seemingly innocent question: Why are there firms at all—why not a collection of independent producers and merchants supplying whatever is called for in the market? Firms are, after all, nonmarket administrative organizations. Coase determined that firms spring up to minimize the "transaction costs" of marketing—namely, the costs of drawing up contracts and monitoring their implementation. Coase's idea—that all economic transactions are in fact explicit or implicit contracts and hence that the role of the law in enforcing contracts is crucial to the operations of a market economy—was soon seen as a revelation. Economic institutions (such as corporations) came to be viewed as social devices for reducing transaction costs.

Coase contributed yet another central tenet of law and economics as a unified field of study in his paper *The Problem of Social Cost* (1960). Here he argued that, except for transaction costs, not only could private deals between voluntary agents always accommodate market failures but that "government failures" (that is, those caused by government intervention) were as deleterious as market failures, if not more so. As Coase stated in the paper,

> *Direct governmental regulation will not necessarily give better results than leaving the problem to be solved by the market or firm. But equally, there is no reason why on occasion such governmental administrative regulation should not lead to an improvement in economic efficiency.*

In other words, transaction costs were central to the problem of social welfare, and markets were inherently more efficient than any social intervention devised by governments. Up to this point the accepted neoclassical welfare economics had promoted "perfect competition" as the best of all possible economic worlds. This theoretical market structure comprised a world of many small firms whose product prices were determined by the sum of all their output decisions in relation to the independent demand of consumers. This perfect condition, however, depended on increasing returns to scale which allow firms to cut costs as their businesses expand. The concept of perfect competition therefore assumed that one or more of the small firms must fail. This argument has been known ever since as the Coase theorem, and *The Problem of Social Cost* produced not just law and economics as a speciality study in economics but led to the new institutionalism in industrial organization referred to earlier.

INFORMATION ECONOMICS

Near the end of the 20th century, information economics became an increasingly important specialization. It is almost wholly the legacy of a single article entitled *The Market for 'Lemons': Quality Uncertainty and the Market Mechanism* by George Akerlof (1970). Akerlof asserted that the market for secondhand cars is one in which sellers know much more than buyers about the quality of the product being sold, implying that only the worst cars— "lemons"—reach the secondhand car market. As a result, secondhand car dealers are compelled to offer guarantees as a means of increasing their customers' confidence. A buyer who knows more about a transaction (i.e., the quality of the secondhand car) will be willing to pay more than a buyer who is provided less information about a transaction. For any product or service, therefore, "asymmetric information" (one party to a transaction knowing more than another) can result in "missing markets," or the absence of a marketable transaction. The potency of this idea and its relevance to all sorts of economic behaviour captivated many economists, leading some to connect it with contract theory and principal-agency theory (concerning situations in which a principal hires an agent to carry out instructions but then has to monitor the agent's performance, as in franchising a business). Two or three decades after Akerlof's groundbreaking work, it was abundantly clear that information economics flowed from his underlying idea of asymmetric information, and in 2001 Akerlof, Joseph Stiglitz, and Michael Spence were jointly awarded the Nobel Prize in Economic Sciences for their work in this area.

FINANCIAL ECONOMICS

Although news about the stock market frequently dominates financial journalism, only since the late 20th century was the stock market recognized as an institution suitable for economic analysis. This recognition turned on a changed understanding of the "efficient market hypothesis," which held that securities prices in an efficient stock market were inherently unpredictable—that is, an investment in the stock market was, for all but insider traders, equivalent to gambling in a casino. (An efficient stock market was one in which all information relevant to the discounted present value of stocks was freely available to all participants in the market and hence was immediately incorporated into their buying and selling plans; stock market prices were unpredictable because every fact that made them predictable had already been acted on.) In the famous economists' joke, there is no point in picking up a $10 bill lying on the sidewalk, because if it were real, someone else would already have picked it up.

The growth of financial markets, the deregulation of international capital markets, and the unprecedented availability of financial data gradually undermined the efficient market hypothesis. By the 1990s there had been enough "bubbles" in stock prices to remind economists of the excessive volatility of stock markets (and to prompt Federal Reserve Board chairman Alan Greenspan to point to the market's "irrational exuberance" when share prices hit new peaks late in the decade). The securities markets seemed anything but efficient, a fact demonstrated again in 2008, when the Dow Jones Industrial Average in the U.S. lost nearly 34 percent of its value during the international financial crisis that began in the previous year. In any case, finance is an area where facts can be highly ambiguous but where the number of people desperately interested in the nature of those facts will guarantee the further growth of financial economics.

OTHER FIELDS

There are different schools of thought in economics, each with its own journals and conferences. One, the Austrian school, now rooted in the United States, with leading centres at New York University and George Mason University, originated in the works of Carl Menger, Friedrich von Wieser, and Eugen von Böhm-Bawerk, all of whom emphasized utility as a component of value. Its free market precepts were brought to the United States by Ludwig Mises and the well-known author of *The Road to Serfdom* (1944), Friedrich A. Hayek.

Charles Darwin's influence can be seen in all of the social sciences, and another alternative school, evolutionary economics—like much of the literature in economics, psychology, and sociology—builds on analogies with evolutionary processes. Also drawing heavily on game theory, it is primarily concerned with economic change, innovation, and dynamic competition. This is not, of course, the first time that economists have flirted with Darwinian biology. Both Veblen and Alfred Marshall were convinced that biology and not mechanics offered the road to theoretical progress in economics, and, while this belief in biological thinking died out in the early years of the 20th century, it has returned to prominence in evolutionary economics.

Pairing his critique of central planning with a defence of free markets, Hayek became a sophisticated evolutionary economist whose advocacy of markets drew attention to the weakest element in mainstream economics: the assumption that economic agents are always perfectly informed of alternative opportunities. A follower of Mises and Hayek, American economist Israel Kirzner developed this line of thinking into a unique Austrian theory of entrepreneurship (involving spontaneous learning and decision making at the individual level) that emphasized a tendency toward economic equilibrium.

Yet another school outside the mainstream is Sraffian economics. As an offshoot of general equilibrium theory, Sraffian economics purports to explain the determination of prices by means of the technological relationships between inputs and outputs without invoking the preferences of consumers that neoclassical economists rely on so heavily. Moreover, Sraffian theory is said to recover the classical economic tradition of Smith and Ricardo, which Sraffians believe has been deliberately buried by neoclassical orthodoxy. All of this stems from Piero Sraffa's *The Production of Commodities by Means of Commodities* (1962), whose 100 or so pages have attracted thousands of pages of elucidation, though the true meaning of Sraffian economics still remains somewhat elusive. Be that as it may, Sraffian economics is a good example of the unequal global diffusion of economic specialization. While it is recognized as a minority school of thought in Europe, Sraffian economics is virtually unknown in American academic circles.

Radical economics, including feminist economics, is better characterized by what it opposes than by what it advocates. A glance at the pages of the *Review of Radical Political Economics* and *Feminist Economics* may cause some to wonder if these specialized concerns should even be considered as economics. That question leads back to the notion that economics is what economists do; in that light, heterodox economics, as exemplified by these and similar networks of dissenters, is indeed economics.

Other principal fields in economics include economic history, health economics, cultural economics, economics of education, demographic economics, the study of nonprofit organizations, economic regulation, business management, comparative economic systems, environmental economics, urban and regional economics, and spatial economics.

Economics has always been taught in conjunction with economic history, but the relationship between these two fields has never been an easy one, and to this day economics departments in the United States include economic historians. In most of Europe, however, economists and economic historians are not joined together institutionally. Although economic historians have won Nobel Prizes (Simon Kuznets in 1971, and Robert Fogel and Douglass North in 1993), most economists do not aspire to study in this area.

The growth of public interest in certain areas affects economists as much as other people. It is not surprising, therefore, that environmental economics has been an emerging subfield of economics. Alfred Marshall and his principal student, Arthur Pigou, created the subject of welfare economics around the theme of the negative "externalities" or spillovers (such as pollution) caused by the growth of big business. Should such "diseconomies of scale" be controlled by administrative regulation, or should firms be made to pay for them by having them buy licenses to pollute? Global warming has dramatized the importance of these questions, and the concerns of environmental economics were priorities of applied economists at the start of the 21st century.

In the 1960s the American "war on poverty" and concerns about schooling brought the economics of education to the fore. That was the decade of interest in human capital theory, and since then the growing health bill of Western countries has drawn similar attention to health economics as a specialization. This is unlikely to change in the years to come, and health economics is perhaps the field in the applied economics of the future with the most promising potential.

One might have thought that the same would apply to spatial economics or the economics of location. After all, what could be more important than the location at which economic activity is carried out? How can the marketing of products be studied without paying attention to the role of location? But although spatial economics has a long and rich history of scholarship (including the work of Johann Heinrich von Thünen and

Alfred Weber), it has never attracted the steady interest of economists. Why that is so is unclear.

Lastly, there is the influence from the field of business management. Developments in higher education have fostered the study of economics within business schools (as opposed to maintaining distinct departments of economics). This trend has been encouraged by the institutions that hire new economists, such as banks, brokerage firms, and governments. As a result, many colleges and universities have reduced their economics faculties while building up their management faculties. The fields of business administration and business economics have their own gurus, but only a few (such as American economists Herbert Simon and Alfred Chandler) straddle both economics and management. By and large, these are different worlds, and only time will tell whether economics and management will one day merge into some new, more comprehensive subject in the study of business governance. What is certain is that economics will remain a vital branch of knowledge, as central to curricula of universities as it is to the conduct of human interaction, with an ongoing proliferation of new theories, schools, and subfields.

PREMARKET ECONOMIC SYSTEMS

Considering the many cultural arrangements that have characterized human society, one would think that there would be a great variety of economic systems, or ways in which humankind has arranged for its material provisioning. Surprisingly, that is not the case. Although a wide range of institutions and social customs have been associated with the economic activities of society, only a very small number of basic modes of provisioning can be discovered beneath this variety. Indeed, history has produced only three such kinds of economic systems: those based on the principle of tradition, those centrally planned and organized according to command, and the rather small number (historically speaking) in which the central organizing form is the market.

The very paucity of fundamental modes of economic organization calls attention to a central aspect of the problem of economic "systems": namely, that the objective to which all economic arrangements must be addressed has itself remained unchanged throughout human history. Simply stated, this unvarying objective is the coordination of the individual activities associated with provisioning—activities that range from providing subsistence foods in hunting and gathering societies to administrative or financial tasks in modern industrial systems. What may be called "the economic problem" is the orchestration of these activities into a coherent social whole—coherent in the sense of providing a social order with the goods or services it requires to ensure its own continuance and to fulfill its perceived historic mission.

Social coordination can in turn be analyzed as two distinct tasks. The first of these is the production of the goods and services needed by the social order, a task that requires the mobilization of society's resources, including its most valuable, human effort. Of nearly equal importance is the second task, the appropriate distribution of the product. This distribution not only must provide for the continuance of a society's labour supply (even slaves had to be fed) but also must accord with the prevailing values of different social orders, all of which favour some recipients of income over others— men over women, aristocrats over commoners, property owners over nonowners, or political party members over nonmembers. In standard textbook treatments, the economic problem of production and distribution is summarized by three questions that all economic systems must answer: (1) What goods and services are to be produced? (2) How are goods and services to be produced and distributed? (3) For whom are the goods and services to be produced and distributed?

All modes of accomplishing these basic tasks of production and distribution rely on social rewards or penalties of one kind or another. Tradition-based societies depend largely on communal expressions of approval or disapproval. Command systems utilize the open or veiled power of physical coercion or punishment or the bestowal of wealth or prerogatives. The third mode— the market economy—also brings pressures and incentives to bear, but the stimuli of gain and loss are not usually within the control of any one person or group of persons. Instead, the incentives and pressures emerge from the "workings" of the system itself. On closer inspection, those workings turn out to be nothing other than the efforts of individuals to gain financial rewards by supplying the things that others are willing to pay for.

There is a paradoxical aspect to the manner in which the market resolves the economic problem. In contrast to the conformity that guides traditional society or the obedience to superiors that orchestrates command society, behaviour in a market society is mostly self-directed and seems, accordingly, an unlikely means for achieving social integration. Yet, as economists ever since Adam Smith have delighted in pointing out, the clash of self-directed wills in the competitive market environment serves as an essential legal and social precondition for the market system to operate. Thus, the competitive engagement of self-seeking individuals results in the creation

The Egyptian pyramids are a testament to the power of command-based economic systems. Sculpies/Shutterstock.com

of the third, and by all odds the most remarkable, of the three modes of solving the economic problem.

Not surprisingly, these three principal solutions—of tradition, command, and market—are distinguished by the distinct attributes they impart to their respective societies. The coordinative mechanism of tradition, resting as it does on the perpetuation of social roles, is marked by a characteristic changelessness in the societies in which it is dominant. Command systems, on the other hand, are marked by their capacity to mobilize resources and labour in ways far beyond the reach of traditional societies, so that societies with command systems typically boast of large-scale achievements such as the Great Wall of China or the Egyptian pyramids. The third system, that in which the market mechanism plays the role of energizer and coordinator, is in turn marked by a historical attribute that resembles neither the routines of traditional systems nor the grandiose products of command systems. Instead, the market system imparts a galvanic charge to economic life by unleashing competitive, gain-oriented energies. This charge is dramatically illustrated by the trajectory of capitalism, the only social order in which the market mechanism has played a central role. In *The Communist Manifesto*, published in 1848, Karl Marx and Friedrich Engels wrote that in less than a century the capitalist system had created "more massive and more colossal productive forces than have all preceding generations together." They also wrote that it was "like the sorcerer, who is no longer able to control the powers of the nether world whom he has called up by his spells." That creative, revolutionary, and sometimes disruptive capacity of capitalism can be traced in no small degree to the market system that performs its coordinative task.

PREHISTORIC AND PRELITERATE ECONOMIC SYSTEMS

Although economics is primarily concerned with the modus operandi of the market mechanism, an overview of premarket coordinative arrangements not only is interesting in itself but throws a useful light on the distinctive properties of market-run societies. The earliest and by far the most historically numerous of economic systems has been that of primitive society, for which tradition serves as the central means of bestowing order.

The Bedouin are among the few societies that rely on tradition-based economic systems. Aleksandar Todorovic/Shutterstock.com

Such economic forms of social organization are likely to be far more ancient than Cro-Magnon people, although a few of these forms are still preserved by such groups as the Eskimo, Kalahari hunters, and Bedouin. So far as is known, all tradition-bound peoples solve their economic problems today much as they did 10,000 years or perhaps 10,000 centuries ago—adapting by migration or movement to changes in season or climate, sustaining themselves by hunting and gathering or by slash-and-burn agriculture, and distributing their output by reference to well-defined social claims. Elizabeth Marshall Thomas describes this distributive system in *The Harmless People* (1959):

> *It seems very unequal when you watch Bushmen [San] divide the kill, yet it is their system, and in the end no person eats more than the other. That day Ukwane gave Gai still another piece because Gai was his relation, Gai gave meat to Dasina because she was his wife's mother....No one, of course, contested Gai's large share, because he had been the hunter.... No one doubted that he would share his large amount with others, and they were not wrong, of course; he did.*

Besides the shared property that is perhaps the outstanding attribute of these hunting and gathering societies, two further aspects deserve attention. The first concerns their level of subsistence, long deemed to have been one of chronic scarcity and want. According to the still controversial findings of the American anthropologist Marshall Sahlins, this notion of scarcity is not true. His studies of several preliterate peoples found that they could easily increase their provisioning if they so desired. The condition usually perceived by contemporary observers as scarcity is felt by preliterate peoples as satiety; Sahlins describes preliterate life as the first "affluent society."

A second discernible characteristic of preliterate economic systems is the difficulty of describing any part of their activities as constituting an "economy." No special modes of coordination distinguish the activities of hunting or gathering or the procedures of distribution from the rest of social life, so there is nothing in Eskimo or Kalahari or Bedouin life that requires a special vocabulary or conceptual apparatus called "economics." The economy as a network of provisioning activities is completely absorbed within and fully inextricable from the traditional mode of existence as a whole.

CENTRALIZED STATES

Very little is known of the origin of the second of the great systems of social coordination—namely, the creation of a central apparatus of command and rulership. From ancient clusters of population, impressive civilizations emerged in Egypt, China, and India during the 3rd millennium BCE, bringing with them not only dazzling advances in culture but also the potent instrument of state power as a new moving force in history.

The appearance of these centralized states is arguably the single most decisive alteration in economic, and perhaps in all, history. Although tradition still exerted its stabilizing and preserving role at the base of these societies—Adam Smith said that in "Indostan or ancient Egypt…every man was bound by a principle of religion to follow the occupation of his father"—the vast temple complexes, irrigation systems, fortifications, and cities of

ancient India and China and of the kingdoms of the Inca and Maya attest unmistakably to the difference that the organizing principle of command brought to economic life. It lay in the ability of centralized authority to wrest considerable portions of the population away from their traditional occupations and to use their labour energies in ways that expressed the wishes of a ruling personage or small elite.

Herodotus recounts how the pharaoh Khufu used his power to this end:

> *[He] ordered all Egyptians to work for himself. Some, accordingly, were appointed to draw stones from the quarries in the Arabian mountains down to the Nile, others he ordered*

to receive the stones when transported in vessels across the river....And they worked to the number of a hundred thousand men at a time, each party during three months. The time during which the people were thus harassed by toil lasted ten years on the road which they constructed, and along which they drew the stones; a work, in my opinion, not much less than the Pyramids.

The creation of these monuments illustrates an important general characteristic of all systems of command. Such systems, unlike those based on tradition, can generate immense surpluses of wealth—indeed, the very purpose of a command organization of economic life can be said to lie in securing such a surplus. Command systems thereby acquire the wherewithal to change the conditions of material existence in far-reaching ways. Prior to the modern era, when command became the main coordination system for socialism, it was typical of such command systems to use this productive power principally to cater to the consumption or to the power and glory of their ruling elites.

Moral judgments aside, this highly personal disposition of surplus has the further consequence of again resisting any sharp analytic distinction between the workings of the economy of such a society and that of its larger social framework. The methods of what could be termed "economic coordination" in a command system are identical with those that guide the imperial state in all its historical engagements, just as in primitive society the methods that coordinate the activities of production and distribution are indistinguishable from those that shape family or religious or cultural life. Thus, in command systems, as in tradition-based ones, there is no autonomous economic sphere of life separate from the basic organizing principles of the society in general.

PRECONDITIONS FOR MARKET SOCIETY

These general considerations throw into relief the nature of the economic problems that must be resolved in a system of market coordination. Such a system must be distinguished from the mere existence of market-places, which originated far back in history. Trading relations between the ancient Levantine kingdoms and the pharaohs of Egypt about 1400 BCE are known from the tablets of Tell el-Amarna. A thousand years later Isocrates boasted of the thriving trade of Classical Greece, while a rich and varied network of commodity exchange and an established market for monetary capital were prominent features of Classical Rome.

These flourishing institutions of commerce testify to the ancient lineages of money, profit-mindedness, and mercantile groups, but they do not testify to the presence of a market system. In premarket societies, markets were the means to join suppliers and demanders of luxuries and superfluities, but they were not the means by which the provision of essential goods and services was assured. For these purposes, ancient kingdoms or republics still looked to tradition and command, utilizing slavery as a basic source of labour (including captives taken in war) and viewing with disdain the profit orientation of market life. This disdain applied particularly to the use of the incentives and penalties of the market as a means of marshaling labour. Aristotle expressed the common feeling of his age when he declared, "The condition of the free man is that he does not live for the benefit of another." With the exception of some military service, nonslave labour was simply not for sale.

The difference between a society with flourishing markets and a market-coordinated society is not, therefore, merely one of attitudes. Before a system orchestrated by the market can replace one built on obedience to communal or authoritarian pressure, the social orders dependent on tradition and command must be replaced by a new order in which individuals are expected to fend for themselves and in which all are permitted—even encouraged—to improve their material condition. Individuals cannot have such aims, much less such "rights," until the dominant authority of custom or hierarchical privilege has been swept away. A rearrangement of this magnitude entails wrenching dislocations of power and prerogative. A market society is not, consequently, merely a society coordinated by markets. It is, of necessity, a social order with a distinctive structure of laws and privileges.

It follows that a market society requires an organizing principle that, by definition, can no longer be the respect accorded to tradition or the obedience owed to a political elite. This principle becomes the generalized search for material gain—a striving for betterment that is unique to each individual. Such a condition of universal upward striving is unimaginable in a traditional society and could be seen only as a dangerous threat in a society built on established hierarchies of authority. But, for reasons that will be seen, it is accommodated by, and indeed constitutive of, the workings of a market system.

The process by which these institutional and attitudinal changes are brought about constitutes a grand theme—perhaps the grand theme—of economic history

Feudal castle in Jumilhac-le-Grand, France. © Hemis.fr/ SuperStock

from roughly the 5th to the 18th and even into the 19th century in Europe. In terms of political history, the period was marked by the collapse of the Roman Empire, the rise of feudalism, and the slow formation of national states. In social terms, it featured the end of an order characterized by an imperial retinue at the top and massive slavery at the bottom, that order's replacement by gradations of feudal vassalage descending from lord to serf, and the eventual appearance of a bourgeois society with distinct classes of workers, landlords, and entrepreneurs. From the economist's perspective, the period was marked by the breakdown of a coordinative mechanism of centralized command, the rise of the mixed pressures of tradition and local command characteristic of the feudal manor, and the gradual displacement of those pressures by the material penalties and rewards of an all-embracing market network. In this vast transformation the rise of the market mechanism became crucial as the means by which the new social formation of capitalism ensured its self-provisioning, but the mechanism itself rested on deeper-lying social, cultural, and political changes that created the capitalist order it served.

To attempt to trace these lineages of capitalism would take one far beyond the confines of the present subject. Suffice it to remark that the emergence of the new order was first given expression in the 10th and 11th centuries, when a rising mercantile "estate" began to bargain successfully for recognition and protection with the local lords and monarchs of the early Middle Ages. Not until the 16th and 17th centuries was there a "commercialization" of the aristocratic strata, many of whose members fared poorly in an ever more money-oriented world and accordingly contracted marriages with wealthy merchant families (whom they would not have received at home a generation or two earlier) to preserve their social and material status. Of greatest significance, however, was the transformation of the lower orders, a process that began in Elizabethan England but did not take place en masse until the 18th and even the 19th century. As feudal lords became profit-minded landlords, peasants moved off the land to become an agricultural proletariat in search of the best wages obtainable, because traditional subsistence was no longer available. Thus, the market network extended its disciplinary power over "free" labour—the resource that had previously eluded its influence. The resulting social order made it possible for markets to coordinate production and distribution in a manner never before possible.

FEUDALISM

Feudalism, a term that emerged in the 17th century, has been used to describe economic, legal, political, social, and economic relationships in the European Middle Ages. Derived from the Latin word *feudum* (fief) but unknown to people of the Middle Ages, it has been used most broadly to refer to medieval society as a whole, and in this way may be understood as a socio-economic system that is often called manorialism. It has been used most narrowly to describe relations between lords and vassals that involve the exchange of land for military service. Feudalism in this sense is thought to have emerged in a time of political disorder in the 11th century as a means to restore order, and it was later a key element in the establishment of strong monarchies. "Feudalism" also has been applied, often inappropriately, to non-Western societies where institutions similar to those of medieval Europe are thought to have existed. The many ways "feudalism" has been used have drained it of specific meaning, however, and caused some scholars to reject it as a useful concept for understanding medieval society.

THE DEVELOPMENT OF CAPITALISM

The historical development of capitalism may be divided into four stages: mercantilism, commercial capitalism, industrial capitalism, and state capitalism.

FROM MERCANTILISM TO COMMERCIAL CAPITALISM

It is usual to describe the earliest stage of capitalism as mercantilism, the word denoting the central importance of the merchant overseas traders who rose to prominence in 17th- and 18th-century England, Germany, and the Low Countries. In numerous pamphlets, these merchants defended the principle that their trading activities buttressed the interest of the sovereign power, even when, to the consternation of the court, this required sending "treasure" (bullion) abroad. As the pamphleteers explained, treasure used in this way became itself a commodity in foreign trade, in which, as the 17th-century merchant Thomas Mun wrote, "We must ever observe this rule; to sell more to strangers than we consume of theirs in value."

For all its trading mentality, mercantilism was only partially a market-coordinated system. Adam Smith complained bitterly about the government monopolies that granted exclusive trading rights to groups such as

The Corn Exchange from Ackermann's "Microcosm of London."
The Bridgeman Art Library/Getty Images

the East India or the Turkey companies, and modern commentators have emphasized the degree to which mercantilist economies relied on regulated, not free, prices and wages. The economic society that Smith described in *The Wealth of Nations* in 1776 is much closer to modern society, although it differs in many respects, as shall be seen. This 18th-century stage is called "commercial capitalism," although it should be noted that the word *capitalism* itself does not actually appear in the pages of Smith's book.

Smith's society is nonetheless recognizable as capitalist precisely because of the prominence of those elements that had been absent in its mercantilist form.

For example, with few exceptions, the production and distribution of all goods and services were entrusted to market forces rather than to the rules and regulations that had abounded a century earlier. The level of wages was likewise mainly determined by the interplay of the supply of, and the demand for, labour—not by the rulings of local magistrates. A company's earnings were exposed to competition rather than protected by government monopoly.

Perhaps of greater importance in perceiving Smith's world as capitalist as well as market-oriented is its clear division of society into an economic realm and a political realm. The role of government had been gradually narrowed until Smith could describe its duties as consisting of only three functions: (1) the provision of national defense, (2) the protection of each member of society from the injustice or oppression of any other, and (3) the erection and maintenance of those public works and public institutions (including education) that would not repay the expense of any private enterpriser, although they might "do much more than repay it" to society as a whole. And if the role of government in daily life had been delimited, that of commerce had been expanded. The accumulation of capital had come to be recognized as the driving engine of the system. The expansion of "capitals"—Smith's term for firms—was the determining power by which the market system was launched on its historic course.

Thus, *The Wealth of Nations* offered the first precise description of both the dynamics and the coordinative processes of capitalism. The latter were entrusted to the market mechanism—which is to say, to the universal drive for material betterment, curbed and contained by the necessary condition of competition. Smith's great perception was that the combination of this drive and counterforce would direct productive activity toward those goods and services for which the public had the means and desire to pay while forcing producers to satisfy those wants at prices that yielded no more than normal profits. Later economists would devote a great deal of attention to the question of whether competition in fact adequately constrains the workings of the acquisitive drive and whether a market system might not display cycles and crises unmentioned in *The Wealth of Nations*. These were questions unknown to Smith, because the institutions that would produce them, above all the development of large-scale industry, lay in the future. Given these historical realities, one can only admire Smith's perception of the market as a means of solving the economic problem.

Smith also saw that the competitive search for capital accumulation would impart a distinctive tendency to a society that harnessed its motive force. He pointed out that the most obvious way for a manufacturer to gain wealth was to expand his enterprise by hiring additional workers. As firms expanded their individual operations, manufacturers found that they could subdivide complex tasks into simpler ones and could then speed along these simpler tasks by providing their operatives with machinery. Thus, the expansion of firms made possible an ever-finer division of labour, and the finer division of labour, in turn, improved profits by lowering the costs of production and thereby encouraging the further enlargement of the firms. In this way, the incentives of the market system gave rise to the augmentation of the wealth of the nation itself, endowing market society with its all-important historical momentum and at the same time making room for the upward striving of its members.

One final attribute of the emerging system must be noted. This is the tearing apart of the formerly seamless tapestry of social coordination. Under capitalism two realms of authority existed where there had formerly been only one—a realm of political governance for such purposes as war or law and order and a realm of economic governance over the processes of production and distribution. Each realm was largely shielded from the reach of the other. The capitalists who dominated the market system were not automatically entitled to governing power, and the members of government were not entrusted with decisions as to what goods should be produced or how social rewards should be distributed. This new dual structure brought with it two consequences of immense importance. The first was a limitation of political power that proved of very great importance in establishing democratic forms of government. The second, closer to the present theme, was the need for a new kind of analysis intended to clarify the workings of this new semi-independent realm within the larger social order. As a result, the emergence of capitalism gave rise to the discipline of economics.

FROM COMMERCIAL TO INDUSTRIAL CAPITALISM

Commercial capitalism proved to be only transitional. The succeeding form would be distinguished by the pervasive mechanization and industrialization of its productive processes, changes that introduced new dynamic tendencies into the economic system while significantly transforming the social and physical landscape.

The transformative agency was already present in Smith's day, observable in a few coal mines where

Watt's steam engine was a major economic catalyst in the Industrial Revolution. The Bridgeman Art Library/Getty Images

steam-driven engines invented by Thomas Newcomen pumped water out of the pits. The diffusion and penetration of such machinery-driven processes of production during the first quarter of the 19th century has been traditionally called the Industrial Revolution, although historians today stress the long germination of the revolution and the many phases through which it passed. There is no doubt, however, that a remarkable confluence of advances in agriculture, cotton spinning and weaving, iron manufacture, and machine-tool design and the harnessing of mechanical power began to alter the character of capitalism profoundly in the last years of the 18th century and the first decades of the 19th.

The alterations did not affect the driving motive of the system or its reliance on market forces as its coordinative principles. Their effect was rather on the cultural complexion of the society that contained these new technologies and on the economic outcome of the processes of competition and capital accumulation. This aspect of industrialization was most immediately apparent in the advent of the factory as the archetypal locus of production. In Smith's time the individual enterprise was still small—the opening pages of *The Wealth of Nations* describe the effects of the division of labour in a 10-man pin factory—but by the early 19th century the increasing mechanization of labour, coupled with the application of waterpower and steam power, had raised the size of the workforce in an ordinary textile mill to several hundreds; by mid-century in the steel mills it was up to several thousands, and by the end of the century in the railways it was in the tens of thousands.

The increase in the scale of employment brought a marked change in the character of work itself. In Smith's day the social distance between employer and labourer was still sufficiently small that the very word *manufacturer* implied an occupation (a mechanic) as well as an ownership position. However, early in the 19th century William Blake referred to factories as "dark Satanic mills" in his epic poem *Jerusalem*, and by the 1830s a great gulf had opened between the manufacturers, who were now a propertied business class, and the men, women, and children who tended machinery and laboured in factories for 10- and 12-hour stints. It was from the spectacle of mill labour, described in unsparing detail by the inspectors authorized by the first Factory Act of 1802, that Marx drew much of the indignation that animated his analysis of capitalism. More important, it was from this same factory setting, and from the urban squalor that industrialization also brought, that capitalism derived much of the social consciousness—sometimes revolutionary, sometimes reformist—that was to play so large a part in its subsequent political life. Works such as Charles Dickens's *Hard Times* (1854) depicted the factory system's inhumanity and the underlying economic doctrines that supposedly justified it. While these works brought attention to the social problems stemming from industrialization, they also tended to discount the significant improvements in the overall standard of living (as measured by the increases in life expectancy and material comforts) that accompanied modernization. Country life of just a generation earlier had been no less cruel, and in some respects it was more inhuman than the factory system being criticized. Those critics who failed to compare the era of industrialization with the one that immediately preceded it also failed to account for the social and economic progress that had touched the lives of ordinary people.

The degradation of the physical and social landscape was the aspect of industrialization that first attracted attention, but it was its slower-acting impact on economic growth that was ultimately to be judged its most significant effect. A single statistic may dramatize this process. Between 1788 and 1839 the output of pig iron in Britain rose from 68,000 to 1,347,000 tons. To fully grasp the significance of this 20-fold increase, one has to consider the proliferation of iron pumps, iron machine tools, iron pipes, iron rails, and iron beams that it made possible; these iron implements, in turn, contributed to faster and more dependable production systems. This was the means by which the first Industrial Revolution promoted economic growth, not immediately but with gathering momentum. Thirty years later this effect would be repeated with even more spectacular results when the Bessemer converter ushered in the age of steel rails, ships, machines, girders, wires, pipes, and containers. The most important consequence of the industrialization of capitalism was therefore its powerful effect on enhancing what Marx called "the forces of production"—the source of what is now called the standard of living.

The development of industrialization was accompanied by periodic instability in the 18th and 19th centuries. Not surprisingly, then, one side effect of industrialization was the effort to minimize or prevent economic shocks by linking firms together into cartels or trusts or simply into giant integrated enterprises. Although these efforts dampened the repercussions of individual miscalculations, they were insufficient to guard against the effects of speculative panics or commercial convulsions. By the end of the 19th century, economic depressions had become a worrisome and recurrent problem, and the Great Depression of the 1930s rocked the entire capitalist world. During that debacle, gross national product (GNP) in the United States fell by almost 50 percent, business investment fell by 94 percent, and unemployment rose from 3.2 to nearly 25 percent of the civilian labour force. Economists have long debated the causes of the extraordinary increase in economic instability from 1830 to 1930. Some point to the impact of growth in the scale of production evidenced by the shift from small pin factories to giant enterprises. Others emphasize the role of miscalculations and mismatches in production. And still other explanations range from the inherent instability of capitalist production (particularly for large-scale enterprises) to the failure of government policy (especially with regard to the monetary system).

FACTORY SYSTEM

The factory system of manufacturing, which began in the 18th century, is based on the concentration of industry into specialized—and often large—establishments. The system arose in the course of the Industrial Revolution.

The factory system replaced the domestic system, in which individual workers used hand tools or simple machinery to fabricate goods in their own homes or in workshops attached to their homes. The use of waterpower and then the steam engine to mechanize processes such as cloth weaving in England in the second half of the 18th century marked the beginning of the factory system. This system was enhanced at the end of the 18th century by the introduction of interchangeable parts in the manufacture of muskets and, subsequently, other types of goods. This advance signaled the onset of mass production, in which standardized parts could be assembled by relatively unskilled workmen into complete finished products.

The resulting system, in which work was organized to utilize power-driven machinery and produce goods on a large scale, had important social consequences: formerly, workers had been independent craftsmen who owned their own tools and designated their own working hours, but in the factory system, the employer owned the tools and raw materials and set the hours and other conditions under which the workers laboured. The location of work also changed. Whereas many workers had inhabited rural areas under the domestic system, the factory system concentrated workers in cities and towns, because the new factories had to be located near waterpower and transportation (alongside waterways, roads, or railways). The movement toward industrialization often led to crowded, substandard housing and poor sanitary conditions for the workers. Moreover, many of

(continued on next page)

(continued from previous page)

the new unskilled jobs could be performed equally well by women, men, or children, thus tending to drive down factory wages to subsistence levels. Factories tended to be poorly lit, cluttered, and unsafe places where workers put in long hours for low pay.

Two major advances in the factory system occurred in the early 20th century with the introduction of management science and the assembly line. Scientific management, such as time-and-motion studies, helped rationalize production processes by reducing or eliminating unnecessary and repetitious tasks performed by individual workers.

The main advance in the factory system in the latter part of the century was that of automation, in which machines were integrated into systems governed by automatic controls, thereby eliminating the need for manual labour while attaining greater consistency and quality in the finished product. Factory production became increasingly globalized, with parts for products originating in different countries and being shipped to their point of assembly. As labour costs in the developed countries continued to rise, many companies in labour-intensive industries relocated their factories to developing nations, where both overhead and labour were cheaper.

FROM INDUSTRIAL TO STATE CAPITALISM

The perceived problem of inherent instability takes on further importance insofar as it is a principal cause of the next structural phase of the system. The new phase is often described as state capitalism, because its

The Great Depression hit previously bustling New York City particularly hard. Archive Holdings, Inc./Getty Images

outstanding feature is the enlargement in size and functions of the public realm.

At the same time, the function of government changed as decisively as its size. Already by the last quarter of the 19th century, the emergence of great industrial trusts had provoked legislation in the United States (although not in Europe) to curb the monopolistic tendencies of industrialization. Apart from these antitrust laws and the regulation of a few industries of special public concern, however, the functions of the federal government were not significantly broadened from Smith's vision. Prior to the Great Depression, for example, the great bulk of federal outlays went for defense and international relations, for general administrative expense and interest on the debt, and for the post office.

The Great Depression radically altered this limited view of government in the United States, as it had earlier begun to widen it in Europe. The provision of old-age pensions, relief for the hungry and poor, and relief for the unemployed were all policies inaugurated by the administration of Pres. Franklin D. Roosevelt, following the example of similar enlargements of government functions in Britain, France, and Germany.

Thus, one very important element in the advent of a new stage of capitalism was the emergence of a large public sector expected to serve as a guarantor of public economic well-being, a function that would never have occurred to Smith. A second and equally important departure was the new assumption that governments themselves were responsible for the general course of economic conditions. This was a change of policy orientation that also emerged from the challenge of the Great Depression. Once regarded as a matter beyond remedy, the general level of national income came to be seen by the end of the 1930s as the responsibility of government, although the measures taken to improve conditions were on the whole timid, often wrong-headed (such as highly protectionist trade policies), and only modestly successful. Nonetheless, the appearance in that decade of a new economic accountability for government constitutes in itself sufficient reason to describe capitalism today in terms that distinguish it from its industrial, but largely unguided, past.

There is little doubt that capitalism will continue to undergo still further structural alterations. Technological advances have reduced to near insignificance the once-formidable barriers and opportunities of economic geography. Among the startling consequences of this technological leveling of the world have been the large displacements of high-tech manufacturing from Europe and North America to the low-wage regions of Southwest Asia, Latin America, and Africa. Another change has been the unprecedented growth of international finance to the point that, by the beginning of the 21st century, the total value of transactions in foreign exchange was estimated to be at least 20 times that of all foreign movements of goods and services. This boundary-blind international-ization of finance, combined with the boundary-defying ability of large corporations to locate their operations in low-wage countries, poses a challenge to the traditional economic sovereignty of nations, a challenge arising from the new capabilities of capital itself.

A third change again involves the international economy, this time through the creation of new insti-tutions for the management of international economic trade. A number of capitalist nations have met the challenges of the fast-growing international economy by joining the energies of the private sector (including organized labour) to the financial and negotiating pow-ers of the state. This "corporatist" approach, most clearly evident in the organization of the Japanese economy, was viewed with great promise in the 1980s but in the 1990s was found to be severely vulnerable to opportunistic behaviour by individuals in both the public and the private sectors. Thus, at the onset of the 21st century, the consensus on the economic role of government in capitalism shifted back from the social democratic interventionism of the Keynesian system and the managed market economies of the "Asian tigers" (countries such as Hong Kong, Singapore, Malaysia, and South Korea that experienced rapid growth in the late 20th century) to the more noninterventionist model of Adam Smith and the classical economists.

It is not necessary, however, to venture risky predictions concerning economic policy. Rather, it seems more useful to posit two generalizations. The first emphasizes that capitalism in all its variations continues to be distinguished from other economic systems by the priority accorded to the drive for wealth and the centrality of the competitive mechanism that channels this drive toward those ends that the market rewards. The spirit of enterprise, fueled by the acquisitive culture of the market, is the source of the dynamism of capitalism. The second generalization is that this driving force and constraining mechanism appear to be compatible with a wide variety of institutional settings, including substantial variations in the relationships between the private and public sectors. The form of capitalism taken also differs between nations, because the practice of it is embedded within cultures; even the forces of globalization and the threat of homogenization have proved to be more myth than reality. Markets cater to national culture as much as national culture mutates to conform to the discipline of profit and loss. It is to this very adaptability that capitalism appears to owe its continued vitality.

CRITICISMS OF CAPITALISM

Advocates and critics of capitalism agree that its distinctive contribution to history has been the encouragement of economic growth. Capitalist growth is not, however, regarded as an unalloyed benefit by its critics. Its negative side derives from three dysfunctions that reflect its market origins.

THE UNRELIABILITY OF GROWTH

The first of these problems is already familiar from the previous discussion of the stages of capitalist development. Many critics have alleged that the capitalist system suffers from inherent instability that has characterized and plagued the system since the advent of industrialization. Because capitalist growth is driven by profit expectations, it fluctuates with the changes in technological or social opportunities for capital accumulation. As opportunities appear, capital rushes in to take advantage of them, bringing as a consequence the familiar attributes of a boom. Sooner or later, however, the rush subsides as the demand for the new products or services becomes saturated, bringing a halt to investment, a shakeout in the main industries caught up in the previous boom, and the advent of recession. Hence, economic growth comes at the price

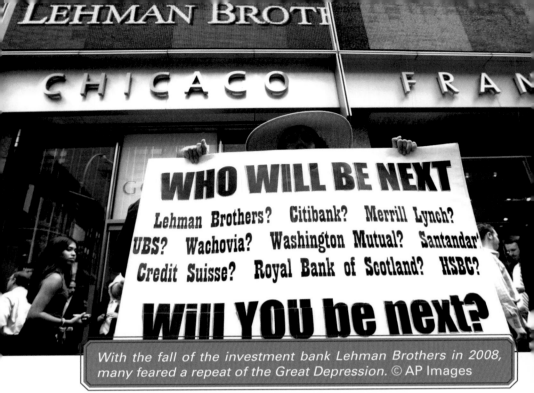

WHO WILL BE NEXT

Lehman Brothers? Citibank? Merrill Lynch?
UBS? Wachovia? Washington Mutual? Santandar
Credit Suisse? Royal Bank of Scotland? HSBC?

Will YOU be next?

With the fall of the investment bank Lehman Brothers in 2008, many feared a repeat of the Great Depression. © AP Images

of a succession of market gluts as booms meet their inevitable end.

This criticism did not receive its full exposition until the publication of the first volume of Marx's *Das Kapital* in 1867. For Marx, the path of growth is not only unstable for the reasons just mentioned—Marx called such uncoordinated movements the "anarchy" of the market—but increasingly unstable. Marx believed that the reason for this is also familiar. It is the result of the industrialization process, which leads toward large-scale enterprises. As each saturation brings growth to a halt, a process of winnowing takes place in which the more successful firms are able to acquire the assets of the less successful. Thus, the very dynamics of growth tend to concentrate capital into ever-larger firms. This leads to still more massive disruptions when the next boom ends, a process that terminates, according to Marx, only when the temper of the working class snaps and capitalism is replaced by socialism.

Beginning in the 1930s, Marx's apocalyptic expectations were largely replaced by the less-violent but equally disquieting views of the English economist John Maynard Keynes, first set forth in his influential *The General Theory of Employment, Interest, and Money* (1936). Keynes believed that the basic problem of capitalism is not so much its vulnerability to periodic saturations of investment as its likely failure to recover from them. He raised the possibility that a capitalist system could remain indefinitely in a condition of equilibrium despite high unemployment, a possibility not only entirely novel (even Marx believed that the system would recover its momentum after each crisis) but also made plausible by the persistent unemployment of the 1930s. Keynes therefore raised the prospect that growth would end in stagnation, a condition for which the only remedy he saw was "a somewhat comprehensive socialization of investment."

THE QUALITY OF GROWTH

A second criticism with respect to market-driven growth focuses on the adverse side effects generated by a system of production that is held accountable only to the test of profitability. It is in the nature of a complex industrial society that the production processes of many commodities generate "bads" as well as "goods"—e.g., toxic wastes or unhealthy working conditions as well as useful products.

The catalog of such market-generated ills is very long. Smith himself warned that the division of labour, by routinizing work, would render workers "as stupid and ignorant as it is possible for a human creature to become," and Marx raised the spectre of alienation as the social price paid for subordinating production to the imperatives of profit making. Other economists warned that the introduction of technology designed to cut labour costs would create permanent unemployment. In modern times much attention has focused on the power of physical and chemical processes to surpass the carrying capacity of the environment—a concern made cogent by various types of environmental damage arising from excessive discharges of industrial effluents and pollutants. Because these social and ecological challenges spring from the extraordinary powers of technology, they can be viewed as side effects of socialist as well as capitalist growth. But the argument can be made that market growth, by virtue of its overriding obedience to profit, is congenitally blind to such externalities.

EQUITY

A third criticism of capitalist growth concerns the fairness with which capitalism distributes its expanding wealth or with which it shares its recurrent hardships. This criticism assumes both specific and general forms.

The specific form focuses on disparities in income among layers of the population. In the early 21st century in the United States, for example, the lowest fifth of all households received only about 5 percent of total after-tax income, whereas the topmost fifth received 53 percent, and the top 1 percent of households received 17 percent. Significantly, this disparity results from the concentration of assets in the upper brackets. Also, the disparity is the consequence of highly skewed patterns of corporate rewards that typically give, say, chief executive officers of large companies more than 300 times the income than those of ordinary office or factory employees. Income disparities, however, should be understood in perspective,

San Francisco labour unions protest in the Occupy San Francisco movement against job cuts. Justin Sullivan/Getty Images

as they stem from a number of causes. In its 1995 annual report the Federal Reserve Bank of Dallas observed,

> *By definition, there will always be a bottom 20 percent, but only in a strict caste society will it contain the same individuals and families year after year.*

Moving from specific examples of distribution to a more general level, the criticism may be broadened to an indictment of the market principle itself as the regulator of incomes. An advocate of market-determined distribution will declare that in a market-based society, with certain exceptions, people tend to be paid what they are worth—that is, their incomes will reflect the value of their contribution to production. Thus, market-based rewards lead to the efficiency of the productive system and thereby maximize the total income available

DISTRIBUTION OF WEALTH AND INCOME

The distribution of wealth and income refers to the way in which the wealth and income of a country are divided among its population or to the way in which the wealth and income of the world are divided among countries. Such patterns of distribution are discerned and studied by various statistical means, all of which are based on data of varying degrees of reliability.

Wealth is an accumulated store of possessions and financial claims. It may be given a monetary value if prices can be determined for each of the possessions; this process can be difficult when the possessions are such that they are not likely to be offered for sale. Income is a net total of the flow of payments received in a given time period. Some countries collect statistics on wealth from legally required evaluations of the estates of deceased persons, which may or may not be indicative of what is possessed by the living. In many countries, annual tax statements that measure income provide more or less reliable information. Differences in definitions of income—whether, for example, income should include payments that are transfers rather than the result of productive activity, or capital gains or losses that change the value of an individual's wealth—make comparisons difficult.

Gross national income (GNI) per capita provides a rough measure of annual national income per person in different countries. Countries that have a sizable modern industrial sector have a much higher GNI per capita than countries that are less developed. In the early 21st century, for example, the World Bank estimated that the per-capita GNI was approximately $10,000 and above for the most-developed countries but was less than $825 for the least-developed countries. Income also varies greatly within countries. In a high-income country such as the

United States, there is considerable variation among industries, regions, rural and urban areas, females and males, and ethnic groups. While the bulk of the U.S. population has a middle income that is derived largely from earnings, wages vary considerably depending on occupation.

for distribution. This argument is countered at two levels. Marxist critics contend that labourers in a capitalist economy are systematically paid less than the value of their work by virtue of the superior bargaining power of employers, so that the claim of efficiency masks an underlying condition of exploitation. Other critics question the criterion of efficiency itself, which counts every dollar of input and output but pays no heed to the moral or social or aesthetic qualities of either and which excludes workers from expressing their own preferences as to the most appropriate decisions for their firms.

CORRECTIVE MEASURES

Various measures have been taken by capitalist societies to meet these criticisms, although it must be recognized that a deep disagreement divides economists with respect to the accuracy of the criticisms, let alone the appropriate corrective measures to be adopted if these criticisms are valid. A substantial body of economists believe that many of the difficulties of the system spring not from its own workings but from well-meaning attempts to block or channel them. Thus, with respect to the problem of instability, supporters of the market system believe that capitalism, left alone as much as possible, will naturally corroborate the trend of economic expansion that has marked its history. They also expect that whatever instabilities appear tend quickly to correct themselves, provided that government plays a generally passive role. Market-oriented economists do not deny that the system can give rise to qualitative or distributional ills, but they tend to believe that these are more than compensated for by its general expansive properties. Where specific problems remain, such as damage to the environment or serious poverty, the prescription often seeks to utilize the market system itself as the corrective agency—e.g., alleviating poverty through negative income taxes rather than with welfare payments or controlling pollution by charging fees on the outflow of wastes rather than by banning the discharge of pollutants.

Opposing this view is a much more interventionist approach rooted in generally Keynesian and welfare-oriented policies. This view doubts the intrinsic momentum or reliability of capitalist growth and is therefore prepared to use active government means, both fiscal and monetary, to combat recession. It is also more skeptical of the likelihood of improving the quality or the equity of society by market means and, although not opposing these, looks more favourably on direct regulatory intervention and on specific programs of assistance to underprivileged groups.

Despite this philosophical division of opinion, a fair degree of practical consensus was reached on a number of issues in the 1950s and '60s. Although there are differences in policy style and determination from one country to the next, all capitalist governments have taken measures to overcome recession—whether by lowering taxes, by borrowing and spending, or by easing interest rates—and all pursue the opposite kinds of policies in inflationary times. It cannot be said that these policies have been unqualified successes, either in bringing about vigorous or steady growth or in ridding the system of its inflationary tendencies. Yet, imperfect though they are, these measures seem to have been sufficient to prevent the development of depressions on the order of the Great Depression of the 1930s—though some recessions, particularly the Great Recession of 2008–09 (the worst economic downturn since the Great Depression) have been enormously destructive. It is not the eradication but the limitation of instability that has been a signal achievement of all advanced capitalist countries since World War II. It should be noted, however, that these remedial measures have little or no international application. Although the World Bank and the International Monetary Fund make efforts on behalf of developing countries, no institution exists to control credit for the world (as do the central banks that control it for individual nations); no global spending or taxing authority can speed up, or hold back, the pace of production for industrial regions as a whole; no agency effectively oversees the availability of credit for the developing nations or the feasibility of the terms on which it may be extended. Thus, some critics of globalization contend that the internationalization of capitalism may exert destabilizing influences for which no policy corrective as yet exists.

A broadly similar appraisal can be made with respect to the redress of specific threats that emerge as unintended consequences of the market system. The issue is largely one of scale. Specific problems can often be redressed by market incentives to alter behaviour (paying a fee for returning used bottles) or, when the effect is more serious, by outright prohibition (bans on child labour or on dangerous chemical fertilizers). The problem becomes less amenable to control, however, when the market generates unintended consequences of large proportions, such as traffic congestion in cities. The difficulty here is that the correction of such externalities requires the support and cooperation of the public and thereby crosses the line from the economic into the political arena, often making redress more difficult to obtain. On a still larger scale, the remedy for some problems may require international agreements, and these often raise conflicts of interest between the country generating the ill effects as a by-product of its own production and those suffering from the effects. The problem of acid rain originating in one country but falling in another is a case in point. Again the economic problem becomes political and its control more complicated.

A number of remedies have been applied to the distributional problems of capitalism. No advanced capitalist country today allows the market to distribute income without supplementing or altering the resulting pattern of rewards through taxes, subsidies, welfare systems, or entitlement payments such as old-age pensions and health benefits. In the United States, these transfer payments, as they are called, amount to some 10 percent of total consumer income; in a number of European countries, they come to considerably more. The result has been to lessen considerably the incidence of officially measured poverty.

Yet these examples of successful corrective action by governments do not go unchallenged by economists who are concerned that some of the "cures" applied to social problems may be worse than the "disease." While admitting that the market system fails to live up to its ideal, these economists argue that government correctives and collective decision making must be subjected to the same critical scrutiny leveled against the market system. Markets may fail, in other words, but so might governments. The stagflation of the 1970s, the fiscal crises of some democratic states in the 1980s, and the double-digit unemployment in western Europe in the 1990s set the stage for the 21st century by raising serious doubts about the ability of government correctives to solve market problems. Events such as the European sovereign debt crisis that began in 2009 only raised more doubts.

CENTRALLY PLANNED SYSTEMS

No survey of comparative economic systems would be complete without an account of centrally planned systems, the modern descendants of the command economies of the imperial past. In sharpest possible contrast to those earlier tributary arrangements, however, modern command societies have virtually all been organized in the name of socialism—that is, with the function of command officially administered on behalf of an ideology purported to serve the broad masses of the population.

Socialist central planning needs to be differentiated from the idea of socialism itself. The latter draws on moral precepts of concern for the needy that can be discovered in the Judeo-Christian tradition and derives its general social orientation from Gerrard Winstanley's Diggers movement during the English Civil Wars in the mid-17th century: "The Earth," Winstanley wrote, "was made by Almighty God to be a Common Treasury of livelihood to the whole of mankind…without respect of persons."

Socialism as a means of orchestrating a modern industrial system did not receive explicit attention until the Russian Revolution in 1917. In his pamphlet *The State and Revolution*, written before he came to power, Vladimir Lenin envisaged the task of coordinating a socialist economy as little more than delivering production to central collecting points from which it would be distributed according to need—an operation requiring no more than "the extraordinarily simple operations of watching, recording, and issuing receipts, within the reach of anybody who can read and who knows the first four rules of arithmetic." After the revolution it soon became apparent that the problem was a great deal more difficult than that. The mobilization of human capital required the complex determination of appropriate amounts and levels of pay, and the transportation of foodstuffs from the countryside posed the awkward question of the degree to which the "bourgeois" peasantry would have to be accommodated. As civil war raged in the country, these problems intensified until production fell to a catastrophic 14 percent of prewar levels. By the end of 1920, the economic system of the Soviet Union was on the verge of collapse.

To forestall disaster, Lenin instituted the New Economic Policy (NEP), which amounted to a partial restoration of capitalism, especially in retail trade, small-scale production, and agriculture. Only the "commanding heights" of the economy remained in government hands. The NEP resuscitated the economy but opened a period of intense debate as to the use of market incentives versus moral suasion or more coercive techniques. The debate, which remained unresolved during Lenin's life, persisted after his death in 1924 during the subsequent struggle for power between Joseph Stalin, Leon Trotsky, and Nikolay Bukharin. Stalin's rise to power brought a rapid collectivization of the economy. The NEP was abandoned. Private agriculture was converted into collective farming with great cruelty and loss of life; all capitalist markets and private enterprises were quickly and ruthlessly eliminated; and the direction of economic life was consigned to a bureaucracy of ministries and planning agencies. By the 1930s a structure of centralized planning had been put

Joseph Stalin. Library of Congress, Washington, D.C. (neg. no. LC-USW33- 019081-C)

into place that was to coordinate the Russian economy for the next half century.

SOVIET PLANNING

At the centre of the official planning system was the Gosplan (*gos* means "committee"), the top economic planning agency of the Soviet state. Above the Gosplan were the political arms of the Soviet government, while below it were smaller planning agencies for the various Soviet republics. The Gosplan itself was staffed by economists and statisticians charged with drawing up what amounted to a blueprint for national economic activity. This blueprint, usually based on a five- to seven-year period, translated the major objectives determined by political decision (electrification targets, agricultural goals, transportation networks, and the like) into industry-specific requirements (outputs of generators, fertilizers, steel rails). These general requirements were then referred to ministries charged with the management of the industries in question, where the targets were further broken down into specific outputs (quantities, qualities, shapes, and sizes of steel plates, girders, rods, wires, and so forth) and where lower-level goals were fixed, such as budgets for firms, wage rates for different skill levels, or managerial bonuses.

Planning was not, therefore, entirely a one-way process. General objectives were indeed transmitted from the top down, but, as each ministry and factory inspected its obligations, specific obstacles and difficulties were transmitted from the bottom up. The final plan was thus a compromise between the political objectives of the Central Committee of the Communist Party and the nuts-and-bolts considerations of the echelons charged with its execution. This coordinative mechanism worked reasonably well when the larger objectives of the system called for the kind of crash planning often seen in a war economy. The Soviet economy achieved unprecedented rapid progress in its industrialization drive before World War II and in repairing the devastation that followed the war. Moreover, in areas where the political stakes were high, such as space technology, the planning system

Soviet leader Mikhail Gorbachev talks with farm equipment workers at a factory in 1987. © AP Images

was able to concentrate skills and resources regardless of cost, which enabled the Soviet Union on more than one occasion to outperform similar undertakings in the West. Yet, charged with the orchestration of a civilian economy in normal peacetime conditions, the system of centralized planning failed seriously.

Because of its failures, a far-reaching reorganization of the system was set into motion in 1985 by Mikhail Gorbachev, under the banner of perestroika ("restructuring"). The extent of the restructuring can be judged by these proposed changes in the coordinative system: (1) the scope and penetration of central planning were to be greatly curtailed and directed instead toward general economic goals, such as rates of growth, consumption or investment targets, or regional development; (2) planning done for factory enterprises was to be taken up by factories themselves, and decisions were to be guided by considerations of profit and loss; (3) factory managers were no longer to be bound by instructions regarding which suppliers to use or where to distribute their products but were to be free to buy from and to sell to whomever they pleased; (4) managers were also to be free to hire and—more important—to fire workers who had been difficult to discharge; and (5) many kinds of small private enterprises were to be encouraged, especially in farming and the retail trades.

This program represented a dramatic retreat from the original idea of central planning. One cannot say, however, that it also represented a decisive turn from socialism to capitalism, for it was not clear to what extent the restructured planning system might embody other essential features of capitalism, such as private ownership of the means of production and the exclusion of political power from the normal operations of economic life. Nor was it known to what extent economic perestroika was to be accompanied by its political counterpart, glasnost ("openness"). Thus, the degree of change in both the economic structure and the underlying political order remained indeterminate.

The record of perestroika over the rest of the 1980s was disappointing. After an initial flush of enthusiasm, the task of abandoning the centralized planning system proved to be far more difficult than anticipated, in part because the magnitude of such a change would have necessitated the creation of a new structure of economic (managerial) power, independent of, and to some extent in continuous tension with, that of political power, much as under capitalism. Also, the operation of the centralized planning system, freed from some of the coercive pressures of the past but not yet infused with the energies of the market, rapidly deteriorated. Despite bumper crops, for example, it was impossible to move potatoes from the fields to retail outlets, so that rations decreased and rumours of acute food shortages raced through Moscow. By the end of the 1980s, the Soviet system was facing an economic breakdown more severe and far-reaching than the worst capitalist crisis of the 1930s. Not surprisingly, the unrest aroused ancient nationalist rivalries and ambitions, threatening the dismemberment of the Soviet economic and political empire.

As the Soviet central government gradually lost control over the economy at the republic and local levels, the system of central planning eroded without adequate free-market mechanisms to replace it. By 1990 the Soviet economy had slid into near paralysis, and this condition foreshadowed the fall from power of the Soviet Communist Party and the breakup of the Soviet Union itself into a group of independent republics in 1991.

Attempts to transform socialist systems into market economies began in eastern and central Europe in 1989

MIKHAIL GORBACHEV

(b. March 2, 1931, Privolye, Stavropol region, Russia, U.S.S.R.), Mikhail Gorbachev served as the last president of the Soviet Union (1990–91). After earning a law degree from Moscow State University (1955), he rose through the ranks to become a full Politburo member (1980) and general secretary of the Communist Party of the Soviet Union (1985–91). His extraordinary reform policies of glasnost and perestroika were resisted by party bureaucrats; to reduce their power, Gorbachev changed the Soviet constitution in 1988 to allow multi-candidate elections and removed the monopoly power of the party in 1990. He cultivated warmer relations with the U.S., and in 1989–90 he supported the democratically elected governments that replaced the communist regimes of eastern Europe. In 1990 he was awarded the Nobel Peace Prize. Russia's economic and political problems led to a 1991 coup attempt by hard-liners. In alliance with president Boris Yeltsin, Gorbachev quit the Communist Party, disbanded its Central Committee, and shifted political powers to the Soviet Union's constituent republics. Events outpaced him, and the various republics formed the Commonwealth of Independent States under Yeltsin's leadership. On December 25, 1991, Gorbachev resigned the presidency of the Soviet Union, which ceased to exist the same day.

and in the former Soviet Union in 1992. Ambitious privatization programs were pursued in Poland, Hungary, Germany, the Czech Republic, and Russia. In many countries this economic transformation was joined by a transition (although with varying degrees of success) to democratic forms of governance.

PROBLEMS WITH SOCIALISM

The socialist experiments of the 20th century were motivated by a genuine interest in improving life for the masses, but the results instead delivered untold suffering in terms of economic depravation and political tyranny. Nonetheless, the egalitarian values that inspired the socialist experiments continue to possess great intellectual and moral appeal. And while socialism has proved less attractive than democratic capitalism, many of the most normatively attractive elements of socialism have

A Soviet woman pushes a shopping cart past a nearly empty refrigerator and shelves at a local general food store, October. 19, 1990. © AP Images

been incorporated into democratic systems, as evidenced by public support for spending on social programs.

The chief economic problem of socialism has been the efficient performance of the very task for which its planning apparatus exists—namely, the effective coordination of production and distribution. Some modern critics have declared that a planned economy is impossible—i.e., will inevitably become unmanageably chaotic—by virtue of the need for a planning agency to make the millions of dovetailing decisions necessary to produce the gigantic catalog of goods and services of a modern society. Moreover, classical economists would criticize the perverse incentives caused by the absence of private property rights. Precisely such problems became manifest in the late 1980s in the Soviet Union.

The proposed remedy to the problems of socialism involves the use of market arrangements under which managers are free to conduct the affairs of their enterprises according to the dictates of supply and demand (rather than those of a central authority). The difficulty with this solution lies in its political rather than economic requirements, because the acceptance of a market system entrusted with the coordination of the bulk of economic activity requires the tolerance of a sphere of private authority apart from that of public authority. A market mechanism may be compatible with a society of socialist principles, but it requires that the forms of socialist societies as they now exist be radically reorganized. The political difficulties of such a reorganization are twofold. One difficulty arises from the tensions that can be expected to exist between the private interests, and no doubt the public visions, of the managerial echelons and those of the political regime. The creation of a market is tantamount to the creation of a realm within society into which the political arm of government is not allowed to reach fully.

Another political difficulty encountered in the move from socialism to the market is the impact on the working class. The establishment of a market system as the major coordinator of economic activity, including labour services, necessarily introduces the use of unemployment as a disciplining force into a social order. Under socialist planning, government commands were used to allocate employment and thereby did not permit the hiring or firing of workers for strictly economic reasons. The problem with this was inefficient production, underemployment, and misallocations of labour. The introduction of a market mechanism for labour is, however, likely to exacerbate class tensions between workers and management. Some socialist reformers tried to overcome these tensions by increasing worker participation in the management of the enterprises in which they worked, but no great successes have been reported. Finally, socialist governments will tend to encounter problems when they come to rely on market coordinative mechanisms, because economic decentralization and political centralization have inherent incompatibilities.

The socialist turn from planning toward the market provides a fitting conclusion to this overview of economic systems, for it is apparent that the three ideal types—of tradition, command, and market—have never been attained in wholly pure form. Perhaps the most undiluted of these modes in practice has been that of tradition, the great means of orchestration in prestate economic life. But even in tradition a form of command can be seen in the expected obedience of community members to the sanctions of tradition. In the great command systems of the past, as has been seen, tradition supplied important stabilizing functions, and traces of market exchange served to connect these systems to others beyond their borders. The market system as well has never existed in wholly pure form. Market societies have always taken for granted that tradition would provide the foundation of trustworthiness and honesty without which a market-knit society would require an impossible degree of supervision, and no capitalist society has ever existed without a core of public economic undertakings, of which Adam Smith's triad—defense, law and order, and nonprofitable public works— constitutes the irreducible minimum.

Thus, it is not surprising that the Soviet Union's efforts to find a more flexible amalgam of planning and market were anticipated by several decades of cautious experiment in some of the socialist countries of eastern Europe, especially Yugoslavia and Hungary, and by bold departures from central planning in China after 1979.

All these economies existed in some degree of flux as their governments sought configurations best suited to their institutional legacies, political ideologies, and cultural traditions. All of them also encountered problems similar in kind, although not in degree, to those of the Soviet Union as they sought to escape the confines of highly centralized economic control. After the Soviet Union abandoned its control over eastern Europe in 1989–90, most of that region's countries began converting their economies into capitalist-like systems.

Something of this mixed system of coordination can also be seen in the less-developed regions of the world. The panorama of these economies represents a panoply of economic systems, with tradition-dominated tribal societies, absolute monarchies, and semifeudal societies side by side with military socialisms and sophisticated but unevenly developed capitalisms. To some extent, this spectrum reflects the legacy of 19th-century imperialist capitalism, against whose cultural as well as economic hegemony all latecomers have had to struggle.

Little can be ventured as to the outcome of this astonishing variety of economic structures. A few may follow the corporatist model of the Asian tigers and the economies of the Pacific Rim (a group of Pacific Ocean countries and islands that constitute more than half of the world's population); others may emulate the social democratic welfare states of western Europe; a few will pursue a more laissez-faire approach; yet others will seek whatever method—either market or planned—that might help them establish a viable place in the international arena. Unfortunately, many are likely to remain destitute for some time. In this fateful drama, considerations of culture and politics are likely to play a more determinative role than any choice of economic instrumentalities.

GLOSSARY

capital A stock of accumulated goods, especially at a specified time and in contrast to income received during a specified period.

communism A system in which goods are owned in common and are available to all as needed.

competition The effort of two or more parties acting independently to secure the business of a third party by offering the most favourable terms.

differential calculus A branch of mathematics concerned chiefly with the study of the rate of change of functions with respect to their variables especially through the use of derivatives and differentials.

efficiency Effective operation as measured by a comparison of production with cost (as in energy, time, and money).

feudalism The system of political organization prevailing in Europe from the 9th to about the 15th centuries having as its basis the relation of lord to vassal with all land held in fee and as chief characteristics homage, the service of tenants under arms and in court, wardship, and forfeiture.

free trade Trade based on the unrestricted international exchange of goods with tariffs used only as a source of revenue.

gross domestic product The gross national product excluding the value of net income earned abroad.

incentive Something that incites or has a tendency to incite to determination or action.

inflation A continuing rise in the general price level usually attributed to an increase in the volume of money and credit relative to available goods and services.

interest A charge for borrowed money, generally a percentage of the amount borrowed.

macroeconomics A study of economics in terms of whole systems, especially with reference to general levels of output and income and to the interrelations among sectors of the economy.

market The area of economic activity in which buyers and sellers come together and the forces of supply and demand affect prices.

Marxism The political, economic, and social principles and policies advocated by Karl Marx; especially : a theory and practice of socialism including the labour theory of value, dialectical materialism, the class struggle, and dictatorship of the proletariat until the establishment of a classless society.

mercantilism An economic system developing during the decay of feudalism to unify and increase the power and especially the monetary wealth of a nation by a strict governmental regulation of the entire national economy usually through policies designed to secure an accumulation of bullion, a favourable balance of trade, the development of agriculture and manufactures, and the establishment of foreign trading monopolies.

microeconomics A study of economics in terms of individual areas of activity.

monetary policy The terms set by a central bank for the borrowing and distribution of its government's money.

monopoly Exclusive ownership through legal privilege, command of supply, or concerted action.

oligopoly A market situation in which each of a few producers affects but does not control the market.

recession A period of reduced economic activity.

socialism Any of various economic and political theories advocating collective or governmental ownership and administration of the means of production and distribution of goods.

supply and demand The relationship between the availability of and desire for a product.

BIBLIOGRAPHY

ECONOMICS

Douglas Greenwald (ed.), *The McGraw-Hill Encyclopedia of Economics*, 2nd ed. (1994); and Phillip Anthony O'Hara (ed.), *Encyclopedia of Political Economy*, 2 vol. (1998, reissued 2001), are two accessible sources of reference addressed to students coming to economics for the first time. An accessible overview of the field is Roger E. Backhouse, *The Penguin History of Economics* (2002).

Representative introductory textbooks are Paul A. Samuelson and William D. Nordhaus, *Economics*, 19th ed. (2010); Richard G. Lipsey and K. Alec Chrystal, *Economics*, 12th ed. (2011); and William J. Baumol and Alan S. Blinder, *Economics: Principles and Policy*, 12th ed. (2012).

ECONOMIC SYSTEMS

Historical analysis is presented in Robert L. Heilbroner, *The Making of Economic Society*, 13th ed. (2012). An excellent presentation along more functional lines, well-written but requiring some acquaintance with economic theory, is Frederic L. Pryor, *A Guidebook to the Comparative Study of Economic Systems* (1985).

CAPITALISM

Robert L. Heilbroner, *The Nature and Logic of Capitalism* (1985), treats the social formation of capitalism. Fernand Braudel, *Civilization and Capitalism, 15th–18th Century*,

3 vol. (1982–84, reissued 1992; originally published in French, 1979), is a wide-ranging overview. Nathan Rosenberg and L.E. Birdzell, Jr., *How the West Grew Rich: The Economic Transformation of the Industrial World* (1986, reissued 1999), discusses the Industrial Revolution and the rise of capitalism. John Kenneth Galbraith, *The New Industrial State*, 4th ed. (1985), is a modern classic. Milton Friedman, *Capitalism and Freedom* (1962, reissued 2002); and Milton Friedman and Rose Friedman, *Free to Choose* (1980, reissued 1990), are perhaps the most accessible treatments of economics and public policy from a market-oriented perspective.

SOCIALISM

A history of the debate over the economic feasibility of socialism is available in Don Lavoie, *Rivalry and Central Planning* (1985). A comprehensive reference collection of the main texts in the socialist calculation debate (theoretical comparisons of centrally planned versus free-market economies) can be found in Peter J. Boettke (ed.), *Socialism and the Market: The Socialist Calculation Debate Revisited*, 9 vol. (2000).

Discussions regarding China, eastern Europe, and the Soviet Union are in Andrei Schleifer and Daniel Treisman, *Without a Map: Political Tactics and Economic Reform in Russia* (2000); Jeffrey Sachs, *Poland's Jump to the Market Economy: The Socialist Calculation Debate Reconsidered* (1993, reissued 1999); and Barry Naughton, *Growing Out of the Plan: Chinese Economic Reform, 1978–1993* (1995).

The classic work on the economic history of the Soviet Union is Alec Nove, *An Economic History of the U.S.S.R., 1917–1991*, 3rd ed. (1992). Peter J. Boettke, *Why Perestroika Failed: The Politics and Economics of Socialist Transformation* (1993), discusses systemic problems with the Soviet-type system.

INDEX

V

W